Words of Praise for
Life Is Short—Wear Your Party Pants

"Loretta LaRoche is a force of nature, the nation's favorite stress maven. As brilliant as she is hilarious, Loretta's witty wisdom is grounded in solid science and cutting-edge positive psychology. Her practical advice about wearing your party pants will set you free to claim peace, creativity, humor, and happiness. This is the best self-help book you'll ever read, and it could be the last one you'll ever need."
— **Joan Z. Borysenko, Ph.D.**,
author of *Inner Peace for Busy People*
and *Inner Peace for Busy Women*

*"I loved **Life Is Short—Wear Your Party Pants**. Loretta is the master at using humor to both create a lively and entertaining book, but more important, to make one stop and pay attention to what she's saying. And what she's saying is that we all need to slow down, love more, treat ourselves more kindly, and seize what life has to offer."*
— **Alice D. Domar, Ph.D.**, Assistant Professor of obstetrics, gynecology, and reproductive biology, Harvard Medical School; author of *Self-Nurture*

"I've loved Loretta ever since I first saw her on Public Television. This book is filled with insight, wisdom, and is presented in a humorous, fun way. I loved it."
— **Dr. Wayne W. Dyer**,
author of *10 Secrets for Success and Inner Peace*
and *The Power of Intention*

*Life
Is Short—
Wear Your
Party Pants*

ALSO BY LORETTA LAROCHE

Relax, You May Only Have a Few Minutes Left
Life Is Not a Stress Rehearsal

Please visit Hay House USA: **www.hayhouse.com**
Hay House Australia: **www.hayhouse.com.au**
Hay House UK: **www.hayhouse.co.uk**
Hay House South Africa: **orders@psdprom.co.za**

Loretta's Website: **www.LorettaLaroche.com**

Life Is Short— Wear Your Party Pants

Ten Simple Truths That Lead to an Amazing Life

✳

Loretta LaRoche

HAY HOUSE, INC.

Carlsbad, California

London • Sydney • Johannesburg

Vancouver • Hong Kong

Published and distributed in the United States by: Hay House, Inc., P.O. Box 5100, Carlsbad, CA 92018-5100 • *Phone:* (760) 431-7695 or (800) 654-5126 • *Fax:* (760) 431-6948 or (800) 650-5115 • www.hayhouse.com • *Published and distributed in Australia by:* Hay House Australia Pty. Ltd., 18/36 Ralph St., Alexandria NSW 2015 • *Phone:* 612-9669-4299 • *Fax:* 612-9669-4144 • www.hayhouse.com.au • *Published and distributed in the United Kingdom by:* Hay House UK, Ltd. • Unit 62, Canalot Studios • 222 Kensal Rd., London W10 5BN • *Phone:* 44-20-8962-1230 • *Fax:* 44-20-8962-1239 • www.hayhouse.co.uk • *Published and distributed in the Republic of South Africa by:* Hay House SA (Pty), Ltd., P.O. Box 990, Witkoppen 2068 • *Phone/Fax:* 2711-7012233 • orders@psdprom.co.za • *Distributed in Canada by:* Raincoast • 9050 Shaughnessy St., Vancouver, B.C. V6P 6E5 • *Phone:* (604) 323-7100 • *Fax:* (604) 323-2600

Editorial supervision: Jill Kramer   *Design:* Amy Rose Szalkiewicz

Library of Congress Cataloging-in-Publication Data

LaRoche, Loretta
  Life is short wear your party pants : ten simple truths that lead to an amazing life / Loretta LaRoche.
    p. cm.
  ISBN 1-40190-148-4 (hardcover) • 1-40190-149-2 (tradepaper)
  1. Conduct of life. I. Title.
  BF637.C5 L365 2003
  158.1—dc21

                           2002152701

                      ISBN 1-4019-0149-2

                  07 06 05 04   9 8 7 6
                    1st printing, February 2003
                    6th printing, August 2004

           Printed in the United States of America

To my girlfriends
Myra, Colette, Joan, Susan, Cheryl, Eva,
Barbara, MaryJane, Sloane, Peggy, Annie,
Jean, Ali, and Christianne—
thanks for being there.

CONTENTS

Acknowledgments xi

Introduction xiii

1: **Say Yes to Stress** 1
("An amazing life requires resilience.")

2: **If Not Now, When?** 25
("An amazing life requires living in the moment.")

3: **The Light at the End of the Tunnel** 49
("An amazing life requires optimism.")

4: **It Is What It Is** 69
("An amazing life requires acceptance.")

5: **Laugh It Up!** 83
("An amazing life requires humor.")

6: **Put a Spin on It** 105
("An amazing life requires creativity.")

7: **Too Much of a Good Thing Can Be Too Much** 125
("An amazing life requires moderation.")

8: **Just Show Up** 139
("An amazing life requires responsibility.")

9: **But What Does It All Mean?** 153
("An amazing life requires meaning.")

10: **Join the Party!** 171
("An amazing life requires connection.")

About the Author 189

ACKNOWLEDGMENTS

I wish to thank all the following individuals for their love and support:

To my husband for being there in good and bad times. To my children, Jon, Laurie, and Erik, and their mates and children. To my mother for teaching me to hang in there, and for her sense of humor. To Brian DeFiore, my literary agent, for all his efforts on my behalf. To Joan Boryscnko for introducing me to Reid Tracy, president of Hay House; and to Reid for helping to make this book and its PBS companion possible. And to my business partner/son, Erik, for his devotion, loyalty, and insight. I am blessed to have you all in my life. . . .

INTRODUCTION

When I was growing up, one of my mother's favorite expressions was "You never know." We'd have to clean the house every Saturday, because . . . "You never know." If we were in the midst of enjoying a wonderful meal, we had to make sure there were leftovers, because . . . "You never know." Small pieces of wax paper were saved, along with brown string and empty egg cartons, because . . . well, you know.

I kept trying to understand what it was that we didn't know but needed to know. It was certainly enough to make a child anxious. Maybe that was the point. After all, we *did* have fire drills at school, and we *were* in the midst of the Cold War—we were even taught to hide under our desks in case of nuclear attacks. Or maybe a meteorite was going to hit the earth, which was something that our third-grade science teacher, Mr. Funkhauser, told us could happen.

Maybe my mother knew that something bad was going to happen and we had to get ready. I used to ask her, but she would always counter with, "Someday you'll see." See what? *What* was I going to see?

I could deal with most of it, but I really had a hard time not being able to wear my patent leather shoes until Easter—especially since we had bought them in February. The only thing I was allowed to do was put Vaseline on them so they wouldn't crack. Isn't that a thrill? I kept begging to wear them, but my mother kept giving me the same answer—you know what she said, don't you?

The thing that really pushed me over the edge was the underwear. She always bought me the most hideous underpants. She said that they were on sale and the clerk told her that they wouldn't wear out. Well, I don't know what the clerk thought I was going to be doing—maybe going into a mineshaft and not coming out for a month? Why did they have to be so sturdy? Why couldn't I just have the kind that were pretty and feminine, with little flowers and lace?

Well, my mother finally had a weak moment and bought me a pair. I was ecstatic until she said the usual: that I couldn't wear them often because . . . "You never know." She added that they were going to be my "party pants." That didn't ease the pain. How many parties does a nine-year-old go to? It's not as if I were a movie star or something. So the pants stayed in the drawer surrounded by their ugly step-underpants. I probably got to wear them twice. I still have them; they just don't fit.

As an adult, I now have a much clearer understanding of what "You never know" meant to my mother and why she needed to say it so often. She and my grandparents lived through the Depression and World War II. These folks have been called "The Greatest Generation" due to their amazing resiliency. They were the product of a world in which the economic present was bleak and the future was scary. As a result, my mother's ability to enjoy things fully was tinged with dread and guilt. For example, she had a wonderful set of hand-painted dishes that had been in the family since I was 14. We carried them home from a vacation in Bermuda and almost broke our backs, they were so heavy. They were a 12-piece setting, each hand-painted with a blue cornflower. Each one was different. Now, frankly, I think the whole thing was a little crazy. Who cared about the fact that each one was different? What was going to happen—were we all going to compare plates, and say, "Oh, look, yours doesn't have a stem?"

xv

My mother thought they were incredibly special. And why not? She'd bought them with her hard-earned money, something she pointed out over and over. They sat in the china closet, waiting for those special individuals my mother felt were deserving enough to eat off them. We, the village idiots, weren't good enough to eat on these superior dishes under ordinary circumstances. Every once in a while she'd remind me that she was leaving them to me. For a long time, I really relished the thought. One day, two years ago, she asked, "Do you want the dishes?" I thought, *You must be kidding.* . . . My idea of dinnerware now is some plastic plates to eat takeout on.

I don't think my mother was mean, and I don't think she really thought her family was unworthy of the good plates. She was simply living the life she was taught to live. We all inherit a point of view from our families and our societies that, for better or worse, creates who we are and what we believe. We often inherit concepts about life but don't really understand why.

One of my favorite stories concerns a woman who was in her kitchen preparing a roast beef for dinner. Her young daughter was watching her make the meal, and the girl asked, "Mommy, why did you cut the ends off the roast beef?"

And the mother told her: "Honey, that's just the way you prepare it."

"But why?"

And the mother had to think about it for a second and acknowledged, "You know, I'm not sure why. It's the way my mother did it, and I'm sure she had a good reason."

"Let's ask Grandma."

So the woman called her mother and asked why she cut the ends off the roast beef. The older woman had to admit that she didn't really know why she did it either, but she did it because that's the way *her* mother prepared a roast beef.

So they called the old woman, the child's great-grandmother, who was now in her 90s, and asked her why she cut the ends off the roast beef before cooking it.

"Well," the old lady said, "it's because I didn't have a roasting pan big enough to hold it."

Many of us have inherited a scarcity mentality from our parents; or a mentality that says we shouldn't celebrate and use the good china in our everyday lives. But like the woman who cooked the roast beef, we have to look beyond what we've been brought up with to try to find our own paths to a happy life.

Certainly, we need to save for the future, and not simply waste things or indulge ourselves with material goods we don't need. But we should never wait to celebrate life only on special occasions. And therein lies the message of this book: We need to bring a feeling of celebration into our lives *every day*. We haven't got time to wait. As I often say to my audiences and workshop members about the precariousness of life: "Nobody is getting out of here alive."

When I make this statement, a lot of people laugh, but I also know they're thinking, *Why is she being so morbid? This is supposed to be funny.* And yet, when we truly acknowledge our mortality, we're forced to live in the present because we understand that that's the only thing that's certain. It forces us to focus on the things that are truly important, and allows us to put aside the things that aren't. It reminds us that what we "awfulize" about today will pass. The slow checkout line becomes a walk in the park. The traffic jam becomes a time to hear good music. And two extra hours at work aren't such a trial if you plan to be home in time to kiss your daughter good night.

We have a very short time on this planet, and we waste so many hours not really enjoying what time we have. So many of us seem to be waiting, waiting. . . . Have you ever asked yourself: "What am I waiting for? What needs to be done before I can do the thing I'm postponing? What do I need to have before I can do it, and why?" Or, "Who am I waiting to get permission from?" Believe me, no one's coming to give you permission—they're out having a good time.

Give It Away and You'll Get It Back

My metaphor of wearing party pants is about more than just enjoying the things we have in the moment and not denying ourselves. It's about recognizing that within us we have a lot to give that makes life extraordinarily special. We can show appreciation and concern more often, hug each other with gusto, be more forgiving, and love each other in more profound ways.

Unfortunately, we've gotten away from the spontaneous sharing of these emotions. My family of origin didn't need books or tapes to help them identify how they felt; they didn't need to buy greeting cards with special words to fit an occasion. People *talked* to one another, and they said what they needed to in person, without a great deal of fanfare.

Passion was rampant. Love was having Aunt Ignatzia pinch your cheeks and say, "Saporita" (sweet one). She didn't go to the drugstore to pick up a card that said the same thing yet cost five dollars.

That generation didn't have much money for lavish food, but they enjoyed their meals with passion. They may have had to walk a few miles instead of driving in an air-conditioned car and listening to a CD player, but they were engaged with their surroundings and said hello to the neighbors that they passed on the way. They lived a life of scarcity, but had inner abundance. *We* live a life of abundance, but too many of us live with inner scarcity.

Live a Life Filled with Simple Truths, and Your Party Pants Will Always Fit

Do you remember how, in the days following the tragedy of September 11, there was an incredible outpouring of love and a search for connection? People came together in amazing ways: There were huge lines at hospitals to donate blood, and children were baking cookies and sending cards and gifts to the rescue workers and the families of the victims. People showed one another simple courtesies in a way that seemed extraordinary and, in fact, *was* extraordinary.

But, really, didn't that just reveal that all of us, for once, collectively felt the precariousness and preciousness of life? We were jarred out of our oblivion and shocked into having to focus on the things that were really important. When the everyday stresses seemed petty, we had to pay attention to what life was really about: connection, kindness, empathy, and love.

I've worked in the field of stress reduction for more than 30 years, and I've helped tens of thousands of people find ways to become more relaxed, and embrace joy instead of anxiety and pain.

In the many years I've been doing this, what I've learned both from my studies and from the thousands of people I've worked with along the way is that the human ability to experience joy, and a deep sense of satisfaction, is something much more in our power than most people realize.

We can all access simple truths that have been available throughout the centuries. We're beginning to see that our society's need to steep itself in the theory that "more is better" has led us down a path of feeling disconnected from others and ourselves. When we begin to integrate moderation, responsibility, good humor, optimism, creativity, resiliency, connectedness, and meaning into our lives, we embrace life with dignity and grace. What better way to have a truly amazing life?

1

SAY YES TO STRESS

"An amazing life requires resilience."

I've spent 30 years—a good part of my adult life—as a coach and consultant, advising people on issues related to stress. I've written books; I've done PBS shows; and I'm constantly on the road talking to large groups of people about how to manage their stress levels.

I thank heaven for stress every morning. I mean, if not for stress, I'd be out of work!

But do you know something interesting? *You* should thank heaven for stress every morning, too.

It's a Sign from Above!

In all the years I've been talking about stress, I keep hearing the same things from people: "My life is so stressful I can't stand it!" "What can I do to get rid of stress in my life?" "I'm so stressed out I can't sleep or eat." "Please help me get rid of my stress!" "I have no room for stress in my life!"

The first thing I want people to understand is this: Thank God you have stress in your life. You should be on your knees saying thank you to your stress every day. The only time you're ever going to have a life without stress is when you're dead. I think we should have a little mantra that we say to ourselves: *"Bless this stress; it helps me see that I'm a mess!"*

What is it about our society that's made us think stress is such an enemy? It's all we talk about, isn't it?

I don't know about you, but I'm feeling stressed from listening to everyone *talk* about their stress!

We act as if stress is a horrible by-product of our overwrought society; that stress is a disease that needs to be cured; that stress is something that needs to be eradicated from our lives in order for us to find a healthy and peaceful existence.

But stress isn't something to try to disguise or eradicate. Stress is a signal. When you recognize it, and work *with* it instead of against it, you can learn a lot about what you need to do to be happier and healthier. Stress is actually a blessing that can help you realize when you need to make changes in your life.

Notice the Signals

We should appreciate the fact that our bodies have a way of letting us know that we need to take action. We need to stop, think, and notice what our body is telling us when we're feeling stressed out. Instead of simply getting swept up in the anger and tension that stress brings out in most people, wouldn't it be interesting to try to listen to the signals? Wouldn't it be helpful to notice when we're acting in the irrational ways that stress can sometimes make us act—and do something about it? Shouldn't we understand that stress is a symptom, not a cause?

3

Someone in one of my seminars once told me that when she's feeling great pressure and stress, she yells at her dog. Now, it seems funny when you read it like that, but honestly don't we all do the same things? Don't you yell at your shoes if a lace breaks when you're late for work? Don't you smack your steering wheel when your car won't start? And, in the worst situations, don't you sometimes find yourselves yelling at your kids or your loved ones when, really, the reason you're upset has nothing to do with them?

Why not work toward training ourselves to stop and say: "You know, I just yelled at the dog. It's not like me to do that. And, besides, isn't it idiotic to yell at the dog? She's a dog. She doesn't speak English. She doesn't understand that she's in my way. Most days, she lies there and I don't say anything. Why am I yelling at her today? And is it really her fault?"

Stress signals are everywhere. We yell at the guy on the radio; we act irrationally in traffic; we're furious over the noisy but playful behavior of children; we wonder if there's a plot against us at work; we feel like everyone in line in front of us at the airport showed up just to spite us . . . we get heart palpitations and high blood pressure.

Sometimes we feel incredible bitterness and anger over mundane, repetitive daily tasks: "Why are you putting dishes in the sink after I just washed them?" "I just made the bed! Why are you lying in it?" As if doing those things just once should take care of it.

We need to be vigilant about noticing these symptoms and looking for the reasons why we feel the way we do. We need to recognize the underlying causes and take action. But so often we don't do that. Instead, we look for simple ways to alleviate the symptoms of stress and make ourselves feel better in the short term. But that's a dangerous game: It's like seeing the red signal and the warning lights at the railroad crossing. You can acknowledge that the signal is serious and you'd better slow down. Or you can make a run for it and try to beat the train across the track—of course, if you do that, you stand a good chance of being flattened like a pancake.

If you don't pay attention to the signals, they'll only get bigger and bigger. Instead of yelling at the dog, you'll be yelling at your boss and losing your job. Instead of weak heart palpitations, you'll end up in the cardiac ward. Instead of a mild headache now and then, you'll be debilitated with migraines.

We have to pay attention to the signals and do something. I'm always fascinated by the fact that the Buddhists see suffering as an opportunity for growth, and see pain and pleasure as two sides of the same coin. In a similar way, stress can be the pathway that leads you to a better life—if you follow the road in the right direction.

5

PAY ATTENTION! SOME COMMON SYMPTOMS OF STRESS

Mood Swings: Do you find yourself crying easily? Or experiencing extreme highs and lows?

Inability to Concentrate: Do you find yourself unable to remember recent events or conversations?

Obsessive Behavior: Are you unable to stop drinking? Eating? Working? Shopping?

> **Inability to Sleep:** Do you wake up in the middle of the night with thoughts racing through your head?
>
> **Irritability:** Do the smallest things sometimes make you fly off the handle?
>
> **Isolation:** Do you find yourself backing away from social situations—finding that it's just easier to be alone?

6

The Three Tiers of Stress Reduction

Our society is one that looks for quick fixes—not to mention that it's one in which we all think that we should be able to buy a product that can solve our problems within moments. And since we're all looking so hard for a solution for our discomfort, stress, and tension, the management of stress has become an enormous segment of our economy.

Many consumer products can be nurturing and make you feel better. Scented soaps and candles, pungent incenses, listening to the sounds of running water—all of those things *do* enhance the quality of life for people who like that sort of thing. I happen to love many of those products, and think that having things around me that are soothing and feel and smell good *do* make the day-to-day moments a little bit better.

That said, as a true way to deal with stress in your life, these peripheral aids are like putting on a Band-Aid when you need open-heart surgery. Not to mention that for some people, they could prove to be *added* stressors: What if you can't afford that drawing class? Suppose you went to six stores and couldn't find the lavender de-stressing skin cream that you like so much?

These are superficial things that may, for a few moments, subdue the pain and anxiety—but that's all they are. They are the top tier, if you will, of a pyramid that will help you understand and manage stress.

The middle tier is the one that supports the body and the mind: more substantial therapies and programs that can help your body grow and learn how to care for itself. For example, you might try exercise programs such as yoga or Pilates—or anything that will help strengthen your body and therefore give you more power and resilience. Also, there's massage—which has been proven to have an immediate and powerful effect on the immune system. And, certain sorts of behavioral therapies in which you learn how to stop giving into negativity are also part of the middle tier.

But these two tiers can't stand without the foundation. The core needs to be solid in order for the rest of it to be really helpful. No matter how many candles you light or how many yoga positions you master, you need to build a solid foundation before you can really understand and make good use of the blessing of stress.

So that's what this book is really about: the things in life that are deeply nourishing and help you balance your life and give it power and meaning. Without looking long and hard at the core issues in your life, you're not going to be able to do much about feeling stressed out. You need to ask yourself if you're having fun in your life, and if you have a sense of what's important to you. You need to look for deeper con-

8

nections with people, live with integrity, and find balance and moderation.

If life is to be enjoyed, then you need to really believe that enjoyment is what it's all about. You need to take note of the wonders around you every day. You need to celebrate. In other words, you need to wear your party pants with pride!

KEEP A JOY JOURNAL

A very useful technique for finding your core, and being able to understand stress in your life, is to keep a Joy Journal.

Joy is not about guilt, anger, bitterness, or resentment. It comes from inner peace, the power to give and receive, and the ability to appreciate. It's a feeling of gratitude for the gift of life. Keeping a Joy Journal will help you maintain a feeling of elation, the sense that you're soaring with the eagles instead of scratching in the dirt with the turkeys. Starting out your day by journaling seems to reduce stress considerably.

It makes perfect sense, doesn't it? Most of us start our mornings by reviewing all the things we need to do that day—an endless list of tasks and duties. And we think of all the ways in which every single one of them might go wrong. So we start off by compressing, in advance, all the horrors that could conceivably befall us in the next 15 hours, and suffer all that pain and worry before we've had our morning coffee.

I don't know why it is that we all seem to love to torture ourselves, but we do, don't we? I actually suggest to my workshop attendees that they might want to go out and buy a small whip to self-flagellate at appropriate moments. The visual image can create an inner "ah-ha"— a moment of recognition that helps them see the absurdity of their inner beatings.

Instead of beginning your day in bondage, why not start out with a daily dose of joy? Focus for a few minutes on the good things, the things that make you feel wonderful and beautiful instead of tedious and out of control.

If you have a hard time getting started, try some of these ideas to move you in the right direction:

10

1. Think of people who have really made a positive difference in your life.

2. List three or four things that you do well.

3. Write down at least five things that you like about yourself.

4. Think of a time in which you had so much love in your heart that you thought it would burst.

5. Think of some of the favorite physical activities you enjoyed as a child (swimming, jumping rope, roller skating . . .). List them, and think about ways you might do them again.

6. Think of five qualities you adore in your partner or spouse. Write them down, and tell him or her about them.

7. Think back to a time when you felt supported while going through a challenge. How did this feel, in detail?

8. Remember three times when you felt inner peace and serenity. Can you capture that feeling? Where were you? Why were you feeling so good?

9. Think of someone you might forgive, and how doing so might change your life.

10. Whom do you laugh with the most? Remember a time when you laughed so hard you thought you'd fall over.

There are hundreds of things that give us joy. Start your day with a few of them and begin to honor your life . . . instead of your anxiety.

✽

Why Do We Think So Small?

In a recent workshop that I led, I met a woman who was terminally serious about her towels. To this woman, the subject of towels was as important as the economy is to Alan Greenspan.

She loved her towels. To her, a beautifully stitched, perfectly color-coordinated towel in the kitchen or bathroom was a work of art. She chose her towels the way Julia Child chooses tomatoes. They had to be the right color, texture, and thickness. They needed to be folded and placed in just the right way to look fluffy and inviting. The proper arrangement and selection of her towels meant a lot to her. They clearly made a statement about how she felt about her home, as well as her personal taste and style.

The problem was, her husband didn't have the same aesthetics or priorities. To him, a towel was something you wiped your wet hands on.

When she started talking about this issue in the group, it was clear that it had been seething inside her for years. Suddenly her husband was Attila the Hun because he used one of the "guest" towels to dry his face after a shower. "My God," she said, "how could he show so little consideration?" She once caught him using one of the good kitchen towels to wipe up a spill on the floor.

Now, I don't mean to belittle this woman's problems. In fact, I thanked her for her insight, and for being so amazingly articulate about pointing out something that we all probably do in many ways during the day. That is, we take little things and make them into huge, global problems. Of course those little things (like towels) aren't what's really bothering us; rather, they're the manifestations of larger issues in our lives.

But whatever the reasons, the effect is that we can take something that's as insignificant as a pimple on an elephant's butt and make it into a nuclear conflict.

There was another woman in the group who had a very similar issue with pillows. She collected them— fancy embroidered ones, simple silk ones, all sorts—and she loved to see them strewn around her living room. But her husband—the nerve of him—would occasionally take a nap on the couch and put his head on one of her pillows. Imagine! The grease from his hair would get on the pillow, and it made her nuts.

Now, the two husbands mentioned above could certainly have been more thoughtful about the issues that were important to their wives. And similarly, the wives could have been more mindful of the fact that their obsessions probably made their husbands feel even less important than those hand towels or pillows. But unless they figured out a way to address the fact

13

that they were feeling blind rage toward their husbands over bits of cloth, there was no solution in sight.

To both of these women, I suggested finding a way to make fun of their respective situations to defuse the growing conflict. By making it so serious, they were joining in a power dance with their husbands about whose priorities were more important. I reminded them that it's so much easier to make light of this type of thing. By the end of our workshop, the woman with the pillows decided that she'd buy her husband his *own* pillow—which he could grease up however he wanted! She also fantasized a bit about tour buses that would pull up to her suburban home and pay good money to see her magnificent collection of pillows.

14

The other woman decided that the next time she caught her husband using one of her fancy kitchen towels to wipe up a spill on the floor, she'd get down on her hands and knees and say, "Thank you, great master." That would get his attention!

> *"Being in control of the mind means that literally anything that can happen can be a source of joy."*
> — Mihaly Csikszentmihalyi

We need to look at the amount of energy we spend feeling bad, anxious, and conflicted, and look for the real source. If it's something small, then why are we bothering? We have to ask ourselves: Is it really worth it? Is this pillow worth losing my marriage? Is it worth losing a night's sleep? Is it really worth my attention at all?

If we all took the energy we spend worrying and obsessing over the small stuff, we could experience world peace in one day!

COGNITIVE DISTORTIONS

We often contribute to our feelings of stress and anxiety by not seeing things around us clearly; we get too emotionally attached to a certain way of thinking, or to what our history has been, and we distort reality. Just recognizing the pattern is one of the first steps to successfully managing stress. Do any of these examples of distorted thinking sound like you?

Black-and-White Thinking: There are no shades of gray, and no middle ground. You always head right for the extreme. You're driving over a bridge and get into what appears to be the slowest line and you think, *I never pick the right one!*

15

Rejecting the Positive: You can't accept it when good things happen to you. You give a great performance in a piano recital and think, *Oh, I made a mistake in the third measure.* Or you get a compliment on a job well done and simply rationalize, *Anyone could have done it.* And you really believe that.

Overgeneralizations: You obsess over one negative thing and see it as evidence of a pattern of negativity. You lose a client and then believe: *I can never make this business a success! I don't have what it takes.*

16

Negative Comparisons: You're always looking at other people to discern the ways in which they're better than you are.

Victimization: No matter what the setback, you think it proves that you can never have a decent life, as in: *I missed the bus! See— things like that always happen to me! Nothing ever goes my way.*

Name-Calling: You tend to label yourself with negative thoughts at the drop of a hat.

You spill a drop of soup in your lap and think, *God, I'm such a disgusting slob. I should never go out in public.*

Being Clairvoyant: You know that the outcome of any situation is going to be negative, so why bother? *I'm never going to win that writing contest, so why should I go to the trouble of entering my story?*

"Shoulding" on Yourself: No matter what the situation, you can always think about what you *should* have done, or *should* have said, instead of what really happened. It's a form of blaming yourself for not always being perfect.

17

Finding a Distortion

Here's a great little technique for getting to the heart of distorted thinking quickly. Grab a piece of paper and a pen. Now write down one thing that you really want to accomplish in your life—something very important to you, that you think could improve your life enormously if you could get it done. Some people I've done this exercise with have thought, *I want to improve my marriage, I want to write a novel, I want to find the child I gave up for adoption,* or *I want to get my college degree.*

Okay, once you've done that, start writing down all the reasons you can think of why you'll *never* accomplish what you want. But don't make anything up. Write down those things that your brain is really telling you will prevent you from meeting your goals.

You might conjure up thoughts such as:

- ❋ *I'm not smart enough.*
- ❋ *I'm not talented enough.*
- ❋ *I don't stick with things long enough.*
- ❋ *I don't have what it takes.*
- ❋ *There's too much competition.*
- ❋ *I'm too tired.*
- ❋ *I've always failed before, so why should it go better this time?*

Now, once you've gotten to that stage, you're going to do a 180-degree twist. Your job is to take every one of those negative thoughts or affirmations and refute each one.

You need to look at your sheet of paper, and if it says: "I don't stick with things long enough," you need to become the defense attorney and start thinking of things that prove that you *do* stick with things long enough. What about that time you built the doghouse the kids wanted? That took three weekends of hard work! What about the time you wrote the 50-page report at work? Sure, it took forever, but you got it done.

Soon, these negative thoughts can turn into positive affirmations: "I do *not* always quit in the middle." "I *do* stick with things long enough to complete them." "I *will* finish that novel I've been working on this time!"

Of course, you're never going to change your perceptions right off the bat. But this exercise just might provide a jumping-off place to see the things that stand in your way—and may help you remove those obstacles.

19

Singing the Blues

One of my favorite ways of getting people to see some of their own distortions—and to also help them get a handle on their stress—is to give them unconventional ways to focus on and articulate the things that bug them. One of the most entertaining ways to do that is to have them sing a blues song about whatever's bothering them.

In the workshops I do at the mind-body medical institutes and elsewhere, I get people to stand onstage with me, think of the things in their lives that are inspiring the most horrible stress and anxiety, and really sing out their troubles at the top of their lungs in the form of a blues song. Some really serious stuff comes out, but by the end of it, nobody's laughing harder than the singer.

This exercise takes away the emotional edge, lessens the anxiety, and just might help change your outlook. When you change your perception of a situation, you're better able to solve it.

It's easy, and I ask that you try it for yourself. A blues song is very structured, very simple. It often starts *"Woke up this morning . . . ,"* and then goes off into a litany of all the pain and suffering that the singer has to deal with. It's often about loss and destitution. Sometimes using this simple structure as a device to frame our own thinking about trivial issues can defuse the power that they hold over us.

Here are a few examples of blues songs that were created and sung in a recent seminar of mine:

> *I woke up this morning*
> *They were at it again*
> *Those damn strawberry hulls are in the sink again*
> *I've got the my husband doesn't throw his crap*
>   *away blues . . .*

> *I hate myself this morning*
> *Can't fit in my clothes*
> *My ass grew two sizes this week*

Even fat down in my toes
I've got the bad body-image blues . . .
Can't stop moanin'
About my weight
Even when my husband says I look great.
Got those bad body-image blues
Won't somebody hand me a piece of cake?

I woke up lonely this morning
Went to bed the same way
My fear of commitment is keeping me that way
I got the lonesome blues
The lowdown lonesome blues
Can't find me a baby, no, I just keep
    running away.

21

Woke up this morning
Didn't sleep a wink
My baby's crying
And the trash can really stinks
I change his diaper every hour
And feed him pureed pears
And I don't have five minutes even
    to comb my hair
I've got the new mama martyr blues.

And here's one by the woman I talked about earlier, who had a thing about her pillows:

I woke up this morning
Didn't want to wake up at all
I knew my pillows would be messed up
And dripping with cat hairballs
I've got the pillow perfection blues
It haunts me day and night
I know my pillows aren't aligned
And nothing in life is right.

22

What about Fun?

All we ever seem to do is talk about how much stress we have in our lives, but why doesn't anyone seem to talk about how much *fun* they're having?

I've never heard a single person say, "I'm such a mess; I had too much fun today!" Of course not, because that's a completely illogical statement. Fun cancels out stress. The chemistry of fun reduces our anxiety levels and roots us in the moment—and when we're living in the present, it allows the mind to stop the incessant demands that lead to our feeling stressed.

Perhaps a way to counter the negative aspects of stress is to give yourself permission to spend equal amounts of time on positive pursuits. If you spend ten minutes worrying about how much work is still piled up on your desk, spend ten minutes thinking about swimming in the lake this coming weekend. If you spend half an hour obsessing about how bad the traffic is and how you're going to be late for dinner, spend a half hour listening to your favorite piece of music and just loving every minute of it.

My mother used to always say to me, "You can have fun when your chores are done." And isn't that the way we all seem to be living our lives? We don't allow ourselves to have fun until all the menial tasks have been taken care of.

23

But guess what? Our chores are never done. And they never will be. Welcome to the real world! A life without stress is a life without challenge and passion.

Don't wait! Incorporate fun into as many moments as you can. At the end of your life, your eulogy should feature a list of all the wonderful things you did for yourself and others. No one will care how many closets you cleaned or how many times along the way you emptied your in-box. *Celebrate often!* No matter how much stress you might be feeling, pull on those party pants and realize that stress is just another part of the wonderful adventure called *life!*

❋ ❋ ❋

2

IF NOT NOW, WHEN?

"An amazing life requires living in the moment."

So many of us spend big chunks of our day—sometimes even weeks at a time—oblivious to the reality of the moments that make up our lives. We spend the bulk of our time inside our head, so wrapped up in our thoughts about the past and our plans for the future that we don't even pay attention to the little things that are happening around us right now. It's as if the present is nothing but a rehearsal for some imagined future performance.

Picture the woman in the supermarket who's walking down the aisle doing the grocery shopping: In her mind, she begins to catastrophize about what all of this means. She's already taken those groceries home, put them away, used them to cook meals that her family has devoured, and she's right back here on another shopping trip, damn it!

She stands there feeling angry and resentful, thinking, *Why the hell am I doing this when I'm just going to have to come back here and do it again next week? Been here, done this. Now I have to do it again, and I'm never going to stop doing this. It's like supermarket purgatory! I'm one of the damned, trapped in the deli line with a number no one will ever call.*

Then her thoughts start to gain some speed: *If I didn't have to waste all my time going to the supermarket like this, then life would be good. I'm much too important to be doing insignificant things like this with my time. I need to be checking my e-mail and doing my paperwork and discussing the nuances of my relationships.*

If this woman isn't living in the moment, *when* is she going to live? The fact of the matter is that the little things are never going to stop. That's life. Life *is* the supermarket trip—it's a series of small events that are wonderful or tragic or annoying or painful or playful. So why doesn't she stand in line and wonder at the bounty of things around her? Why not appreciate her ability to taste and smell? Why not beam with pride as she takes in the realization that she can *afford* the groceries she's about to buy?

Rabbi Abraham Joshua Heschel once said, "Time is the dimension wherein we become aware that every instant is an act of creation," and "authentic existence

26

requires work and celebration, ritual and prayer, and an appreciation of the nature of time."

Every moment is "the" moment—good, bad, and indifferent. It's what you're doing; it's the life you're living. To deny it, and live alternatives inside your head, is to deny your very existence.

La-La Land

Remember when you were a kid and you got into "heavy staring," and your mother would say, "Hey? Where are you? Come back! Are you in la-la land?"

As an adult, you've probably buried or dismissed this wonderful place that can help you find inner peace and harmony. Children daydream often and with great ease because they have the capacity to focus on the moment they're living in.

If children see a kite, a balloon, a bird, or anything else that strikes their fancy, they're able to zero in on it and track it with complete absorption. It's as if the child has become *one* with the object.

This becomes harder and harder to do as our minds become more and more cluttered with adult demands. How often have you sat down for a few moments to chill out, and then heard that nagging little inner voice starting in on you: *What are you doing, just sitting there?*

27

You don't have time for this! Get up. You have lots to accomplish today! Snap out of it!

Children don't have those voices in their heads yet. That's why we have to keep hounding them to do things like clean their room, pick up their toys, and watch where they're walking. They're so wrapped up in the delightful, adventurous activities that they're focused on that it's no wonder parents find themselves constantly saying things like, "I'm talking to you! Listen!" It's as if we're desperately trying to break the spell, even if just for a minute.

But we grownups can learn to be spellbound again—to connect to "la-la land." It's not about writing one more report or answering a few more e-mails—but rather about getting more in touch with the universe.

You see, when we're in concert with something or someone we love, we're in a state of "flow," where time and space become nonexistent, our moments expand, and we're literally one with the universe. Our minds become free-floating, unattached to our everyday concerns—and our bodies release the tensions that often make us look like dead parrots.

I find that my garden draws me into this other world. When I'm there, I transcend time and space and let go of my cares and concerns for a while. You can get to "la-la land," too. Just take some time to meditate, pray, journal, walk in nature, spend time with a loved one, or any activity that takes you to that magical place where time stands still.

Welcome to Nirvana!

Living in the moment has become more available to us in the last several years through the many books and tapes on Buddhism that have flooded the market. One of the cornerstones of Buddhism is meditation, which trains the mind to still its inner chatter so that it can become more available to a loving, peaceful life. Buddhists also seem to understand the ultimate irony that the very nature of being alive brings with it a fair amount of suffering.

If we could fully understand and embrace this truth, then every painless moment would be one in which we would resonate with joy, since we'd have a profound understanding that the very next moment might be one in which we truly suffer. But our Western minds find this to be a very difficult task, since our culture has taught us to rely on heavy doses of magical thinking and instant gratification. How many times have we said, "If only this would end, then I could be happy," "When I go on vacation, I'll feel better," or "I can't wait till Friday"? We even have a restaurant chain that uses the tag line "Thank God It's Friday." Why can't we say "Thank God It's Monday"? Living our lives as if Friday is the ultimate day of relief sets us up to miss all the joyful opportunities that a Thursday, a Wednesday, or, yes, even a Monday, might bring.

> *"I have an existential map; it has*
> *'you are here' written all over it."*
>
> — Steven Wright

30

Have you ever sat around planning for what you hope will be a great vacation? You gather tons of brochures with pictures of magnificent haciendas, palm trees, Olympic-sized pools, and pristine lagoons. In your mind, you're picking native fruits off the vines and letting the juice run down your chest. You're basking in perfect weather, eating scrumptious foods, and having magnificent sex . . . (probably *any* sex would be great, because most of the time you're generally too busy to even think about it).

But when you arrive, what happens? You find that the brochure photos were taken 20 years ago when the resort was first built. Now half of it has been closed, the pool is empty, the lagoon's been shut down thanks to pollution, and the septic tank has backed up. And sitting in front is an old toothless hag with a sign that says: WELCOME TO NIRVANA!

How many of our life experiences end up like that? The anticipation is so much greater and takes so much more time than the reality. For example, you take a new job because you're dissatisfied with your old one. You're in the new place three weeks and there's a "reorganization"—your corner office suddenly becomes a cubicle, you find that your 401(k) is worthless, and your "expense account" gives you enough funds to buy lunch at McDonald's once a month.

Or, you purchase the home of your dreams and find killer mold in the basement. Within six months, it's worth more as a penicillin factory than as a house. Or, you think you've found the person of your dreams and you're blissful that you've finally met your soulmate. Then you go to the post office to mail out the wedding invitations . . . and you see your intended's picture on an "FBI's Most Wanted" poster.

None of this rhetoric is meant to negate the fact that our futures may hold great promise and joy. It's the future that gives our dreams viability and helps keep the candle of hope burning brightly. But when we spend too much time using our hopes for the future as a way to take us away from the realities of the present, we turn our expectations into disappointments.

31

TRY THESE SIMPLE EXERCISES

❀ Wake up every day and shout, "I'm back!" (if you're living with someone, tell them, too).

❀ On weekdays, pretend you're on a "working vacation," and appreciate every moment of the day.

❀ Tell at least three people at work how happy you are to be breathing.

32

Quick, Give Them What They Want

It's often impossible to be focused on the "here-and-now," simply because the mind seems to have . . . a mind of its own. We all have subpersonalities that bubble up throughout the day, giving us instructions on how or what we should be doing. Many of them are compilations of parents, significant others, siblings, co-workers, and ourselves; and it's often difficult to distinguish one voice from another. Their one common denominator is that they intrude and try to tell us all the things we *ought* to be doing or thinking—for example: *God, do I ever have a lot to do! I need to get back to the office. I feel so fat. I'd better finish my lunch—it's horrible to waste food. I really need to buy cat litter on the way home.* Sound familiar?

And this continues, for most of us, throughout virtually everything we do over the course of a day. The voices may be berating us with negativity, or they can be reminding us of positive things. It doesn't really matter. The point is, they take us away from what's happening around us.

Imagine yourself taking a soul-stirring walk through a mountain path that meanders by a breathtaking crystal-blue lake. You hear the soothing sound of the water lapping against the shore; and the sweet music of birds playing, crickets chirping, and leaves rustling in the wind. Yet you completely undermine the joy of the moment by taking yourself away from it, psychologically. You lose the majesty and peaceful nature of the scene due to the chatter in your head—chatter that has absolutely nothing to do with the beauty surrounding you, and everything to do with stress from the outside world. You think, *What time is it? If I don't get that promotion and raise, I'm going to have to quit! I can't afford a new roof on the house right now. What am I going to do?* So instead of having a lovely, rejuvenating walk through nature, you've created an opportunity to add to your burden of stress, anxiety, and panic. Because when you're *thinking* it, you're *feeling* it.

33

It's not surprising that staying focused and mindful has become so foreign to us. Particularly in the last few years, all we've heard is how important it is to multitask! If we're not doing five different things at once in this society, then we're not productive enough. We should be driving our car, talking on the phone, making notes on our Palm Pilot, listening to the stock market reports on the radio, and reading the newspaper—all at the same time. It's crazy.

Nothing is simple and focused anymore. When we buy a camera, it also chops vegetables; our telephones are typewriters. Nothing in our world these days contributes to serenity and focus.

34

I used to like to watch the news. Have you turned on CNN lately? It's impossible to find the newscaster in all the chaos that's on the screen. There's a scroll across the bottom and another one along the side. You have to read and listen at the same time—usually about separate subjects. It makes me crazy! I'm constantly distracted: If I read the scroll, I lose track of what the newscaster is saying; if I listen to the newscaster, I'll find myself drawn to one phrase crawling across the bottom of my screen, like "Giant alien pod discovered in the middle of Wal-Mart" and think, *God, I'd better pay attention to that!*—but too late, it's gone.

Do all of these voices and their demands for our attention contribute to making us better informed, or do they simply make us more distracted and less able to focus on one thing at a time? I think it contributes to the overall rudeness in our society—a feeling that we don't have to pay full attention to anyone at any time. In fact, doesn't the world all around us feel more and more like a television tuned to *Headline News?*

Stop the Chatter

Think of the effect that all the chatter in your head has on a conversation. Conversation is about *communication*—about mutual give-and-take, about listening to someone else, and being heard yourself. It's actually a very deep and personal form of bonding, isn't it? Except for sex, conversation is probably the most intimate way for two human beings to communicate. Think of the basis of the very word *communicate*—"commune."

But when the dialogue going on inside your own head becomes a cacophony of voices telling you what to do, how can you possibly concentrate on what the other person is saying? You can't! You take what should be a moment in which two people bond together, and instead make it a narcissistic moment that's all about you. So, even though you're talking to somebody else, you're really having a conversation with yourself that the other person is intruding upon!

35

Life becomes so much richer and more meaningful when we can truly be present—not only to ourselves,
but to others as well.

STOP THE DANCE OF CHAOS!

The art of being present is somewhat paradoxical: We must learn to acknowledge the chatter and its demands, while at the same time hold
on to being in the here-and-now. Not an easy
task—but one that can be learned with practice.
Keep in mind that Buddhist monks spend their
entire lives practicing what's commonly known
as *mindfulness meditation*, and even they attest to
how difficult it can be.

When your mind begins its dance of
chaos, simply acknowledge it by saying something like: "Oh, well. There you go again.
Yes, I hear you." If you saw the movie *A
Beautiful Mind,* you'll recall that one of the
ways the main character helped control the
hallucinations his schizophrenic mind was
creating was to acknowledge them, even
though he knew they weren't real. Try the
same technique on yourself. Listen to the
voices and acknowledge them. Then return to
focusing on where you are.

36

Respecting the Moment

Think about all the times in your life you've berated yourself for doing something wrong. I bet that most of those instances weren't particularly serious—that is, they weren't life-threatening or particularly harmful to anyone—but the level of self-flagellation was brutal. Many of us just seem to be heavily invested in beating ourselves up and feeling guilty about everything. That's why they call guilt "the gift that keeps on giving."

It's important to realize that some guilt is useful; after all, it helps form a conscience. Guilt is helpful in stopping us from being unethical in our business relationships or mean-spirited toward those we love. But leaving dishes in the sink or not making the beds doesn't fall in the same category. Ruminating over such mundane situations accomplishes nothing. Unless, of course, they create an Academy Award for the most guilt—then at least we'd have something to put on our mantel.

37

Think for a moment of the hundreds of different ways you make yourself feel bad throughout the day. Trust me, I've done it more than most—I learned this dynamic well. I had great teachers, starting with my grandmother, who used to wear black all the time . . . *just in case somebody died.*

There are a lot of things that bring out the guilt in me, but some are more powerful than others. Trying to lose weight always elicits major self-flagellation. I usually start well in advance of the actual process of shedding pounds by spending a few months torturing myself with how awful I look and continually asking myself, *How did this happen?!* The answer is obvious . . . I ate too much. But that doesn't seem to quiet the monster of self-loathing that many of us are familiar with.

My voices continue in an inspired chorus: *You're getting older—what do you expect? What happened to that 24-inch waist—it's now your thigh measurement, isn't it? I wonder what year you'll fit into that size six you used to wear? Maybe they can put it on you when you're dead.* Then when I'm actually invested in some type of program, the voices remind me that I didn't exercise enough, even if I ran a 27-mile marathon; or that maybe I should eat less, even though I just finished a meal consisting of a lettuce leaf washed down with a bottle of water.

Similarly, my friend Shirley always talks about how she should have stayed later at work to catch up—even though her overtime is starting to exceed the amount of hours she was actually hired to work. I know from some of Shirley's co-workers that she spends a lot of time at the office talking about her feelings of guilt. In some ways, this type of drama gives us a form of negative validation—but it saps our energy and devours our spirit. Now, if Shirley spent the same amount of time on the task at hand, she'd probably go home early. And I've finally realized (it takes me a long time) that if I spent as much time walking as I do *talking* about losing weight, I'd be a recovering anorexic. . . .

Only when we become conscious of how and what we say to ourselves can we truly be fully present. The ancient Persian poet Rumi said it well when he said that we should wake up, for we've been asleep for thousands of years.

39

AN ANTI-GUILT EXERCISE

When the guilty chatter starts rattling around in your head, counter those voices with an assertive comeback. Say, "Look, I may have had some failures in life, but I'm a survivor. Some inner strengths got me to this place, and I'm sure they'll get me even farther." Write down your strengths in your Joy Journal . . . and refer to the list often.

"Don't Think about the Position"

When I took my first yoga class many years ago, my teacher was an older gentleman named Raj. He was then about 65 years of age, but his lean, muscular frame and spirit did not show it. In fact, the very first time I came to Raj's house, his wife answered the door and led me to the backyard . . . where her husband was hanging upside down from a swing. Raj quickly and gracefully leapt to the ground, shook my hand, and gave me a most splendiferous grin. An incredible sense of peace came over me, and I knew that I'd found someone who was going to be quite instrumental in the direction my life would take.

I decided to take private lessons with him, even though it was at a time in my life when I could hardly afford it. I wanted desperately to learn everything this man could offer me, so I went into my study of yoga with intensity. My nature is to want to excel at everything I do—and that has been both my cure and my curse. During my first few classes with Raj, all I cared about was whether or not I was executing the poses properly. He'd strike a pose and gently ask me to execute it, while his lovely, soft, melodious voice reminded me to breathe and then stretch, breathe and stretch . . . I'd try desperately to imitate what he did, holding my breath in my attempt to get it right. After all, wasn't everything about getting it right? What if I looked ridiculous or didn't breathe right or my leotard hiked up?

And as Raj noticed this, he came over and commented, "It's not about the positions, Loretta. Let go and breathe, and it will come. Inhale, exhale. *Be here now!*"

I remember thinking that he was nuts. How could I ever learn anything by just breathing in and out? Letting go? How does a major control freak let go? I didn't have a clue what that even meant. To me, the concept meant that I might fall into a big black hole and never get out. It sounded very weird. (Keep in mind that this was at least 30 years ago. We weren't in the place we're in now, where yoga has become a national pastime.) Of course, the point of Raj's lesson was: Stop thinking about all the other stuff that gets in the way. But that's an incredibly difficult thing to do. Until you get the false expectations and the other negative chatter out of your head, you'll never accomplish your goals.

41

JUST BREATHE

When you find yourself losing touch with the moment, just concentrate on nothing else but your breathing for a while. Close your eyes (if possible), and simply feel yourself inhale,

> then exhale—focus on the breath as it comes
> in and out. You'll be surprised how easily this
> will clear your mind and allow you to focus on
> what's really happening around you, as it also
> helps you to "be here now."

Try to Go Out of Your Mind

There are times when life's complications make our
inner chatter harder to control. We all know by now
that the voices in our heads are often so relentless that
nothing seems to quell them.

There's a great body of research stating that exercise in and of itself can elevate mood as it distracts one
from the mayhem of the mind. I mean, it's pretty hard
to listen to your inner chatter and play tennis at the
same time. If you do something physical with your
body, your head will clear. After all, you're not a mind
and a body . . . but a mind/body. One is witness to the
other, and together, they become the judge and jury to
your way of life.

I play racquetball. I can't very well be running
around the court, trying to make a play, watching to
make sure a ball isn't going to hit me in the face—and
still have time to think about paying the bills. For that

hour, I'm living in the moment. And when the hour is over, my head is clearer.

There are a variety of healthy distractions that can make us return to the present with more clarity and focus. I know, I know, I've been telling you to *not* distract yourself up until now. But keep in mind that the mind is often paradoxical. There's something about our ability to change focus and *consciously* distract ourselves with positive things that makes the chatter lessen. Try it—it works!

When you're obsessing about a problem at work or how heavy your thighs have gotten, start doing some jumping jacks. Play some music that you love. If you have a pet, take it for a walk (unless it's a snake . . .). If you're lucky enough to have grandchildren, spend the day with them. You get the point.

43

Cool Your Jets

I'm always amused by how impatient everyone has become. No one wants to wait for anything anymore. Merchants are trying to provide services as quickly as possible, yet people still complain when it takes more than five minutes to get a burger and fries.

In fact, this whole thing began with the concept of "fast food." We became enthralled with the ability to get an entire meal in less than the 20 minutes or so it would have taken in a restaurant. Now that most people's lives have become nothing more than an endless to-do list, every retailer imaginable has gotten on the bandwagon, and God forbid if it takes more than 30 seconds to accomplish anything.

You can get your dry cleaning done in less than 24 hours—even though it may have the dirt of 20 years embedded in the material. Your eyeglass prescription can also be filled in 20 minutes. Cholesterol screening takes five minutes—and you can have it done while you're training your dog not to poop on the rug.

44

You can have your thighs reshaped during lunch, and your breasts lifted while you're having dinner. If that's not to your liking, you can have a mini-tuck at your local gas station while you're filling your tank and buying groceries for dinner.

You can do psychotherapy while driving to work—you merely pick up your therapist and take him with you. They pick your brain while *you* pick on the other drivers who aren't going fast enough to suit your accelerated mind.

Television sets now come with screens within screens so we can watch two shows at once. We spend our lives clicking away, erasing voice mails and e-mails faster than the eye can see. Who cares if we miss something? We don't want to waste any time; we're much too important!

We have to hurry up and get rid of all this mundane stuff so we can get on with the important stuff. Like what? The reality is, of course, that whatever we do at any given moment is, in fact, our life! We will not get do-overs. There is no repeat performance.

We're all becoming so invested in this hurry-up mentality. But the bottom line is: Not everyone is a paramedic. Unless you've got someone in cardiac arrest in the back of your car . . . slow down when you come to a tollbooth.

Then take a deep breath and pay for the person behind you. It could extend your life.

45

The Lights Are On, but Nobody's Home

One of the greatest downfalls of "non-presence" is that many of us live as if we're on automatic pilot. In this state, our minds are shrouded in a dense fog, plowing ahead without our even knowing where we're headed or why.

For example: Many of us obsess over our diet, yet we gobble down our food in three minutes while driving our cars or talking on our cell phones.

The best way for us to get a handle on what we eat is to eat *mindfully*. Here's a great exercise: Can you, for just one dinner, stay completely focused on what you're putting in your mouth and nothing else? Try it!

Savor the moment—the flavor, the smell, the texture, the way the food feels as it travels to your stomach. In the beginning, it will be easier to do this if you're alone and not talking to others, but that will become possible with practice.

With each bite, really get into the sensuality of it. Feel it in every way possible. Don't think about work, the kids, or your mother-in-law. Don't think about how much time this exercise is taking. Don't think about the amount of calories you're ingesting. Just savor the moment. Chew each bite fully, luxuriously. Take your time and concentrate on what you're doing.

I guarantee you that this will be the best meal you've had in a very long time. I also guarantee you that it will be the healthiest, regardless of what was on your plate. When you eat mindfully, your body has time to react to what you're putting into it. You'll eat more sensibly, and you'll most likely eat an awful lot less than you would otherwise. When you can take the time to really sense what your body is telling you—and what your senses appreciate—your body regulates itself wisely.

When you eat while performing several other tasks, the chance of feeling satisfied is slim to none.

46

Your mind is concentrating on other things, so how could you possibly be truly aware of what you're eating and the effect it's having on your body?

The same is true of everything you do . . . all day, every day. The more you stop the noise and really stay present in what you're doing, the better you're going to do it.

Sex is the obvious illustration. How good is sex when your head's full of chores that have to be done? It's pretty clear that when you're distracted during sex, the pleasure suffers.

We're constantly bombarded with information overload, with dozens of things that need our attention, with a life full of distractions and complications. The ability to keep our minds clear and focused is one of the most critical talents we human beings have. When you find yourself doing things out of habit (or inertia) instead of feeling truly present and engaged in the moment, take a step back and ask yourself: *Why have I chosen not to be here now? Do I really believe that my next moment might be better even though it's an illusion?*

The Talmud asks the question: "If not now, when?" If we don't live our lives now, to the fullest, when in the world will we have the chance? If we don't pay attention to the little wonders of life right this second, when will we be able to?

❋ ❋ ❋

3

The Light at the End of the Tunnel

"An amazing life requires optimism."

Science has proven that people who employ an optimistic attitude tend to live longer and have a stronger immune system. In other words, optimism appears to be a natural antidepressant and mood enhancer.

In uncertain times, the optimist expects the best—while the pessimist thinks that if something can go wrong, it will. I always tell my audiences that pessimists may be more accurate, but they don't live as long. . . .

Some of us may possess a greater propensity toward optimism, while others may naturally lean toward pessimism. But whatever your nature, the ability to bring an optimistic attitude to life can be taught and enhanced.

Just Believe in Yourself—Not!

First, here's what optimism is not. Optimism is not a blind and thoughtless belief that everything's going to be okay no matter what. A lot of motivational gurus would have you believe that all you have to do is think positive thoughts and your problems will disappear. This is an inaccurate way of looking at life. It's simplistic and disrespectful to the complexities of the human experience. For example, what does that say to people who get a debilitating disease? "Well, now that you're ill, you should feel guilty about having the disease. You probably weren't thinking the right thoughts, that's why you're sick"?

Should we tell people who work for a corporation that has suffered a six-billion-dollar loss and is laying off 20,000 employees that if they just believe in themselves, they'll thrive? The implied message here is that if life isn't working out for these individuals, they're just not believing in themselves hard enough.

This isn't optimism. It's insanity.

People who go around thinking that life is always going to go their way if they think positive thoughts aren't optimists—they're idiots. A true optimist wakes up thinking, *Anything could happen today—good or bad. And whatever happens, I can deal with it.*

> *If you think the worst and get the worst, you*
> *suffer twice, if you think the best, and get the*
> *worst, you suffer once. . . ."*
> — Anonymous

Optimists Know That the Bad Comes with the Good

Optimists know that there are bad things that can happen, and they accept that that's the way it goes. They don't ignore the pitfalls of life, but rather, understand that they exist—and then don't obsess over them.

Optimists take detours around the pitfalls and keep themselves focused on a possible pleasant outcome. They're not in denial; if they feel an unfamiliar lump in their breast, they immediately make an appointment with a doctor. But where a pessimist might use that discovery as an opportunity to stop engaging in life and sink into a narcissistic obsession over how their life is about to end and how things never go their way, the optimist goes about their business—staying engaged in day-to-day activities, and thinking through the possible positive outcomes of the discovery as well as the negative ones.

Optimists like to act on the illusion that they're in control of their lives, and they *don't give up*. They behave like movie directors—shooting and reshooting a scene until it feels right, and making adjustments to the story as required. They continue to act in ways that they believe might give them the outcome that they hope for. Of course, they walk a fine line, because they *do* understand that they're really not in control—no one is. But for optimists, the ability to act on the illusion that they can shape their future helps them make sense of, and attach hope to, any reality.

In fact, studies suggest that reality is overrated. According to psychiatrist Susan C. Vaughan, author of *Half Empty, Half Full,* "People who are most closely in touch with reality are probably depressed."

As a young girl, my home was rife with arguments; you could cut the tension with a knife. As a result, I often felt frightened and terribly anxious—so my saving grace became my ability to fantasize. I had and still do have an active imagination. I owe a lot to it, and to the fact that I was an avid movie buff. Movies would often become the vehicles for my mind to distract itself from the pain and sorrow I was feeling. I even created a cameraman named Sam. At night, I would put myself to sleep by saying, "Sam, roll the camera."

I was able to get through the dark times by picturing myself as Scarlett O'Hara. And so, I was able to shift myself from the reality (feeling like a victim) to the illusion (that I was a victor).

"The mind is its own place, and in itself, can make a heaven of hell, a hell of heaven."

— John Milton

HOW WE CREATE A PESSIMISTIC LIFE
(Or, Ten Ways to Struggle and Live on the Dark Side)

1. We cut off ties to a network of family or friends—so there's no one to validate, understand, and give us loving support.

2. We lack a connection to a higher purpose.

3. We live in the past (or the future).

4. We become overly critical and judgmental.

5. We always have to have things our way.

6. We have little pleasure, fun, joy, and humor in our life.

7. We're attached to negative patterns and pessimistic thoughts.

8. We never seek inner guidance.

53

9. We have rigid rules, standards, and beliefs.

10. We feel overextended. We have too much to do and consequently, we define ourselves with doing, not being.

"The pessimist sees difficulty in every opportunity. The optimist sees the opportunity in every difficulty."
— Winston Churchill

54

The Use of Explanatory Style

A good technique for reshaping negative thinking into optimistic thinking is to simply look long and hard at the way we talk about life. Researchers have proven that our brain patterns are defined in part by how we think—our brain is deeply affected by our inner dialogues; in fact, the language we use helps us create our ability to think positively or negatively. Optimists take credit for their successes and see bad events as flukes. Pessimists, on the other hand, blame themselves for anything that happens and often discount success.

Have you ever been with someone who just can't say thank you when you give them a compliment—

they'd much rather tell you what's wrong with them? Dr. Martin Seligman has dubbed the dialogue of pessimism and optimism as *explanatory style*. He points to the fact that pessimists use the three P's to explain themselves: *personalization* ("It always happens to me!"), *pervasiveness* ("It happens to me every day in every way!"), and *permanence* ("It will never end!").

This practically guarantees a life that contains a feeling of hopelessness and suffering. It also contributes to a sense of inner worthlessness and a lack of self-control. The more we think we *are* a certain way, the more we *become* that way. If we go around thinking that we're a failure, then before long, no matter what we do, we fail. If we go around thinking that we've been working so hard that we should be tired, it's going to be awfully hard to feel energetic.

55

We can change the way we feel by changing how we think. We all need to learn "how to think about what we're thinking about."

The Optimists' Training Institute

When I help people discover how to become more optimistic, a technique I find useful is to have them look back at their lives and see how they overcame adversity. You see, we've all had difficult junctures in our lives—and for the most part, we survive them and go on. It's the bumps in the road that often give us that "can do" feeling.

When I was a young woman, I opted to get divorced. Up until that time in my life, I hadn't had to work to support myself. I received child support, but I still had to earn a great deal of money to compensate for what was lost. I taught yoga and exercise classes, painted and wallpapered houses, and cooked for a tennis club. Fortunately, the combination of my spirit and the humor I brought to my exercise classes made me exceedingly popular. But when I wanted to add elements of mind/body work to my classes, my bosses balked. And when I came up with the "revolutionary" idea of playing music in my classes, I was fired. So I went out, rented studio space, and started teaching on my own. Before long, I had a following and a business.

56

Looking back on those days now, I feel enormously proud of that young woman who had the wherewithal to take risks, experiment, and take chances on her own ideas, instead of safely drawing a paycheck every week. Take a minute and think about this: Were there times in your life when you faced misfortune and found a way to turn things around? What inner resources did you draw on to get yourself through the tough times?

Optimists are able to create the present and the future by owning and acknowledging the strengths they used to get through the past. To paraphrase Ernest Hemingway, we get strong in the broken places.

HAVE ANY OF THESE STRENGTHS HELPED YOU GET THROUGH TIMES OF ADVERSITY?

Tenacity	Humor
Courage	Reliability
Perseverance	Compassion
Integrity	Resilience
Acceptance	Flexibility
Honesty	Empathy

Optimists also resonate with whatever has given them joy, fun, and humor. What memories can you recall that have brought you great pleasure?

When you think of some, write them down. It may sound corny, but once again, research shows that the very act of recalling such moments may actually enhance our ability to stave off sickness—particularly colds and upper-respiratory illnesses.

Make lists, and keep them in places where you can glance at them—such as your desk at work, next to your telephone at home, or taped to your bathroom mirror. Review them periodically.

For many people, looking at a list of accomplishments or happy events triggers feelings of discomfort. If this happens to you, just sit with it until it passes. Taking ownership of the moments of greatness in your life leaves you room for more. It gives you strength and reminds you of just how resourceful you are. When you have a sense of your own capabilities, it's easier to become optimistic about life in general.

58

BOOST YOUR WORD POWER; BOOST YOUR MOOD

In today's world, we're losing ground in the vocabulary department. While e-mail is quick and efficient, it's downsized our language skills. This is particularly disturbing because our brains are deeply affected by our inner dialogues, and similarly by our language. Choosing different sorts of words changes the patterns in our brains. That's the amazing power of language.

It makes sense intuitively, doesn't it? If someone asks you how you're feeling today, and your answer is always a kind of mindless,

"Oh, fine," how do you think that contributes to the way you feel? It keeps everything on an even, if boring, keel. It rules out enthusiasm, energy, and vitality. It keeps the heat at room temperature. It helps pattern the brain into making sure that, indeed, you feel kind of mindlessly "fine."

But if, instead, you could be really specific and descriptive about the way you feel, it would honor the emotions inside you and help your brain define and respect them. It would give shape to the wide range of your feelings; and the more you understand your feelings and repeat their language, the more you'll give yourself room to feel them. It would fill you with energy and enthusiasm to live life to the fullest—to really *feel* your feelings.

Think about the words you use. Do you act like you're in a vast field of wildflowers, or are you stuck in a ditch?

Here are some wildflower words: *Joyful, delightful, encouraging, challenging, hopeful, creative, insightful, playful, whimsical, relaxing,*

> *amazing, brilliant, caring, thoughtful, amusing, courageous, brave, bold, respectful.*
> **Here are some words to ditch:** *Awful, terrible, horrible, always, never, hopeless, impossible.*

"What does not destroy me, makes me stronger."
— Friedrich Nietzsche

I had an amazing conversation recently with a man who picked me up in an airport taxi. Michael was only in his late 20s, yet he'd lost both his parents just a year or so before. His mother, who'd been bipolar, committed suicide at age 54. His father, a Vietnam vet and lifelong alcoholic, died at 51. Michael hardly ever saw his father while growing up—he'd occasionally stop by, make promises that he wouldn't keep . . . and not visit again for years. Once, when Michael was six years old, his father promised him that he'd come back that fall and take him to a New England Patriots game. Of course, he never showed up.

Now Michael works in the accounting department at a local hospital and sometimes drives for a car service to earn some extra money. He has a wife, and a life full of hope. He told me that he always keeps his word, and that his boss at work gives him more and more responsibility because he knows that whatever happens, Michael will deliver what he promises.

Michael says that he'll never let anyone down the way his father did. It's a betrayal he never forgot, and a lesson he learned about living with other people in the world.

Some people facing the same circumstances might go through life acting on this impulse: *Nobody can be trusted—everybody always lets me down, so why should I keep my promises?* But not Michael. He lives with an optimistic outlook, and he made a conscious choice to learn and grow from his own misfortunes.

61

GO TO THE MOVIES

We're a storytelling species. Human beings learn about the human experience—and about our endless possibilities—through stories. And what more exciting way to be told a story than at the movies? Watching movies that spark an optimistic view of life can help develop positive illusions, and serve as good examples for shifting our own behavior. Some of my favorite films include: *It's a Wonderful Life, Forrest Gump, A Beautiful Mind, Sleepless in Seattle, Shirley Valentine, About a Boy, Pay It Forward, Life Is Beautiful,* and *My Big Fat Greek Wedding.*

Chubby Checker Had the Answer . . . Just Do the Twist!

An essential part of optimism—and one that can be taught—is the ability to see yourself slip into negative thinking, and then turn it around—that is, twist it. This is easier said than done.

You're probably walking around right now with those nagging voices in your head that I call "the committee": the scolding echoes of the past that are always pointing out the things you do wrong. *There are dishes in the sink! Why are you sitting around doing nothing, you lazy slob? Do you really need to eat that cookie? You have no self-control. You're going to be as fat as a house; in fact, you already are! Why don't you just use your behind as a billboard?* The committee can do a lot to ruin your day.

Then on top of what's in your own head are all the day-to-day messages of media and marketing. The mass media is a constant sledgehammer, thwarting a normal person's ability to feel optimistic about life. It's as if our society preys on people's insecurities, doubts, and fears. You're constantly assaulted with marketing gimmicks that make you feel bad about yourself: products that will make you thinner, younger, and more fit; help you earn more money; or find you a better mate.

Of course, the subtext of all of that is that you, just as you are, are pretty hopeless. Unless you're as rich as

62

Oprah Winfrey, as beautiful as Halle Berry, or as fit as Serena Williams, you're not living up to your "full potential." How could you ever be expected to feel optimistic about life in the face of all of that? It often seems as if life is just a struggle to acquire things or improve yourself—in ways that seem completely out of your reach. And then, as if on cue, there's the voice of the committee, telling you that it's all your fault.

Okay, take a deep breath. It's time to twist things around. Try to find the absurdity in your emotions and have a laugh at your own expense. When you find yourself feeling, *Damn, I'm just never going to look like Madonna no matter how many times I go to the gym,* stop and think, *Who cares? She may have great arms and lots of records, but nobody in the whole world has toes like mine. People would come from far and wide to see my toes if they knew how great they were. You know, if the media ever got wind of this, I wouldn't be able to leave my house for days!*

63

When we begin to access the ridiculous, it allows us to stop being so invested in pessimistic thoughts. If traffic always feels like a nightmare to you, once again twist it around. Think about the possibility of being stuck in a traffic jam for days, and how that would give you time to meditate, make phone calls to people you haven't connected to in years, and try out interesting yoga positions you could do in your car. And while you're sitting there, think: *So I don't drive an $80,000 Mercedes SUV, which, according to the ads, I could use to climb to the top of a mountain and hover there among the cloud formations . . . no matter. My Ford Taurus gets me everywhere anyway, and there are so many SUVs and trucks out there that I've finally become totally unique!*

STAND UP TO THE COMMITTEE

When you hear the voice of the committee in your head, with their familiar refrain of *Who do you think you are, acting like you deserve that promotion? You're not smart enough! Admit it!*—hear the voice, stop it in mid-sentence, and recognize it for what it is. Say, "That's not me talking—I don't know who it is, but I don't like it! And I *do* deserve it!

64

Optimists Believe in Hard Work

Optimists realize that the best things in life come from hard work, and they don't resent doing it. Tenacity is a hallmark of these people—they understand that results come from diligence, and they honor the process.

These days, so many of us expect instant results. One of the best examples of this is the idiotic diet traps that so many of us fall into. We're at a 63-percent obesity rate in this country, so obviously the thousands of diet books on the market are missing something. Most of them claim to have concocted a magic combination of foods, which when eaten at the right time of day or night expedite weight loss. I suppose some people feel that they've embarked on some spiritual path since they're denying themselves the things that they love . . . such as real food.

The exercise gadgets also offer quick results. "Just strap it on and it rubs the fat away!" Right—the only thing that will happen is you'll end up with worn-out-looking skin.

65

We all know that it doesn't work that way. The only way to successfully lose weight is to eat moderately and move briskly—no instant gratification is going to work here. After all, you already experienced *that* when you overindulged. . . .

The truth of life, and the hardest thing for most of us to face, is that there are no easy answers. Life is hard work, an endless process, something we have to confront every single day. And the only way to get more out of life is for us to work hard, stay committed, and never give up. In his groundbreaking book *Emotional Intelligence,* Daniel Goleman concluded that our capacity for progress toward goals depends on an ability to tolerate frustration, control impulses, and delay gratification. People who need to have everything they want *right now* (like a two-year-old) are destined for disappointment and failure.

Optimists understand that every step in the right direction takes them one step closer to where they want to be. They choose action over inertia. They understand that hard work pays off, and there are no shortcuts. They have the ability to keep the faith, press on, and stay committed for the long haul. And that's why they tend to get more out of life.

COMPARATIVE SUFFERING

One of the ways we can enhance our feeling of optimism is to compare ourselves to those who are less fortunate. Our mothers somehow seemed to know this without reading the contemporary research. Remember hearing Mom say things like, "Don't be so selfish. There are people out there who have real problems"? It appears that mood is boosted when we view ourselves as better off than someone else. The additional benefit is that any guilt attached to such feelings of superiority often propels us to become more altruistic.

It's from the Inside Out, Not the Outside In

> *"Reflect upon your present blessings, of which*
> *every man has many; not on your past misfor-*
> *tunes, of which all men have some."*
> — Charles Dickens

Optimists understand that the way to improve their lives is to start from the inside out. They still may desire those things that serve to make their lives better, more comfortable, or just give them a thrill. However, they know that nurturing and caring for their internal landscape will, in the end, allow them to rejoice and celebrate life every day.

67

4

IT IS WHAT IT IS

"An amazing life requires acceptance."

When I was younger, I spent a considerable amount of time and energy on what I thought was the noble pursuit of . . . making myself taller.

Yes, I knew all the tricks. I'd spend hours in the beauty parlor having my hair done in a style that was assured to help me look tall—unfortunately, I ended up looking like a pregnant bumblebee. I'd wear shoes with heels so high that I teetered on them precariously. I discovered certain designers whose clothes were carefully crafted with sleek lines to make even bowling balls look slim and lanky. So I'd buy these extra-long pants, which were supposed to make my legs look longer— but all they did was make me trip a lot.

I walked around with constant foot trauma; spent hundreds of extra dollars on my clothes and hair; devoted countless hours of my time to shopping, primping, and fussing; and, of course, I used up enormous amounts of my psychic energy and attention in the pursuit of this illusion.

Guess what? I'm still short.

When I finally gave up trying to convince people that I was really a tall glass of water instead of a shot glass—my life improved enormously. I no longer had to walk around in pain, I could wear whatever clothes I liked, and I wore my hair in more attractive ways. Once and for all, I stopped walking around pretending to be something I wasn't.

70

Acceptance of what is can not only be wonderfully liberating, but it can also create a great deal of inner peace and harmony. That's wonderful—too bad this society tends to be brimming with control freaks. In fact, I have to admit that this has been one of the most difficult struggles in my life. To paraphrase the Serenity Prayer, I must learn to accept the things I cannot change, have the courage to change the things I can, and gain the wisdom to know the difference. Knowing all this doesn't make it easy, however. I'm well versed in acceptance—after all, I've spent years studying ways to reduce stress, and acceptance is at the very core of managing our stressors. Yet not a day goes by that I don't struggle with the urge to change someone or something.

I'll point out to my husband that he should stop eating Raisin Bran every day and try something else, or that he should join an organization so he can be with more people. The interesting thing is that *I'm* the one who gets upset and worn out from noticing and scolding—he's perfectly fine with himself the way he is.

Before you feel too sorry for him, understand that I do the same thing to myself. I look at myself in the mirror and become my own plastic surgeon. I lift and scrunch, and turn to see what difference it would make in my appearance. It's ridiculous, because I'm not going to be able to walk around holding up my body parts like that. I'm of a certain age where things are just not where they used to be. Sure, I could choose to operate, but until I decide to do so, I need to just stop it!

71

*"Living apart and at peace with myself, I came
to realize more vividly the meaning of
the doctrine of acceptance. To refrain from
giving advice, to refrain from meddling in
the affairs of others, to refrain, even though the
motives be the highest, from tampering
with another's way of life—so simple, yet so
difficult for an active spirit. Hands off!"*
— Henry Miller

Self-Improvement, Not Self-Delusion

I'm all for people doing everything they can to improve their lives, but I worry that for many people, the pursuit of self-improvement (when it becomes an obsession) can lead to a life characterized by struggle, disappointment, and depression.

I'd love for human beings everywhere to live a life full of joy, energy, celebration, and fun. I want us all to laugh, enjoy, play, make love, and do all the wonderful things that make life magical and amazing. Every single one of us can live a life that's a joyous romp through a playground of the spirit—if we take the time to focus on the important things in life.

However, many of us have taken the concept of "self-improvement" into the realm of yet another demanding, high-stress job. We spend months reading books, attending seminars, taking classes, and doing therapy—in pursuit of making more of ourselves. For a lot of people, that's a worthy and wonderful pursuit, but for others, it's destructive and depressing. Some people in our "You-can-do-anything!" society simply cannot accept the fact that there are certain things that they're probably better off not doing.

It may be that you simply don't have the body type to be a successful javelin thrower—and you never will. That's all there is to it. But our society says, "Don't

limit yourself! If you want to be a javelin thrower, simply work harder at it. Take more javelin-throwing seminars, write goals for yourself, say daily affirmations, and
before long, you'll be throwing your way to an Olympic
gold medal!"

I say, "Aren't you better off accepting the fact that
you're probably not cut out for javelin throwing, and
instead go toward the things that are your real strengths?
Maybe you're a sprinter, or maybe you're simply not a
gifted athlete, and you should instead be spending your
time studying music, sculpture, or psychology."

Unrealistic expectations—the sort that would convince us that all we need to do to achieve anything is
to just believe in ourselves and never give up—are
ridiculous. No matter how much I believe in myself,
and no matter how much hard work I put into trying
to change things, the fact remains that I'm short, and
I'm always going to be short.

73

In the same vein, we also go out of our way to have
relationships with people who don't serve our best interests. How many of us have fallen in love with someone
who has the characteristics of Freddy Krueger from
A Nightmare on Elm Street? Yet, instead of accepting the
fact that they're no good for us, we take it upon ourselves
to try every trick in the book to turn them into Sir
Laughs-a-Lot. Unfortunately, the joke's on us—but we
don't get to laugh much because we're in too much pain.

Why do we tend to see everything that we can't have or do as some sort of insult to our ego, instead of looking at, accepting, and taking pleasure in the things that we *do* have and the things we *can* do? Why can't we see our own qualities as gifts that don't need to be exchanged?

LOOK AT THE FOLLOWING LIST AND CHECK OFF SOME OF THE GIFTS THAT YOU ALREADY POSSESS

Loving ___	Perceptive ___
Kind ___	Interpretive ___
Compassionate ___	Insightful ___
Funny ___	Structured ___
Agile ___	Organized ___
Strong ___	Theatrical ___
Supple ___	Stable ___
Flexible ___	Innovative ___
Energetic ___	Precise ___
Graceful ___	Generous ___
Tenacious ___	Thoughtful ___
Musical ___	Subtle ___
Artistic ___	Detailed ___
Mathematical ___	Broad-minded ___
Empathetic ___	Creative ___

They Are What They Are

From time to time, we're all faced with situations that make our lives more complex. These can involve family members, friends, or co-workers. I don't know about you, but I've spent a lot of time on these situations. I find myself using too much energy trying to change or manipulate events and people so that they resemble the movie in my mind.

It's often more productive to wish I were taller.

People are what they are. Situations are what they are. I'm not saying that we shouldn't try to improve our lot in life, or that we're powerless to change certain things, but we'll save ourselves a lot of time and disappointment by being realistic about the situation and our expectations for the outcome.

At this point in time, my greatest challenge is to accept the fact that my 90-year-old mother has moved in with me . . . so has her caretaker, Beatrice. My home, which once was my sanctuary, has turned inside out. My mother has daily questions about her medications and doctor appointments; she also has constant anxiety about whether she'll have enough money to live on. She's deathly afraid that she'll end up on the sidewalk somewhere with her belongings. This makes me feel like a combination of primary-care physician and financial advisor.

It also drives me nuts.

My mother and I have always had a very challenging relationship—I've often described her as Joan Crawford sprinkled with a little Leo Buscaglia. It's been the quintessential love/hate relationship.

Mom now suffers from a mild form of Parkinson's disease. She also has a great deal of pain from arthritis. The result is that she's somewhat hunched over, and walking from one room to another is an effort. I offer advice on how and what she could do to feel better, but she doesn't pay attention to me.

76

I'll say, "Why don't you exercise? Go outside and take a walk with Beatrice!"

"Okay, okay," she answers. But she never goes.

My need to fix and change has come full circle. As a child, I saw myself as one of the *Little Women*—which was one of my favorite movies. The mother in that movie was always very sweetly calling her children "Darling." My mother would go outside and scream my name while ringing a bell.

This movie isn't going to turn out the way I envisioned it, nor are the last days of my mother's life going to be *Tuesdays with Morrie*.

"All adversity is really an opportunity
for our souls to grow."

— John Gray

I'm an avid reader of Buddhist philosophy, and if there's one concept that's advocated over and over again, it's the art of acceptance. And so I ask myself: *What will I learn from accepting this situation with my mother, even when I'd give anything not to have it in my life?* In my lucid moments, I recognize the validity of the famous Buddhist saying. "When the student is ready, the teacher appears." And so, I've become witness to my own mortality. I've been given the opportunity to learn to be compassionate to the aging, because I'm on that path myself. In addition, my mother has shown me her ability to be resilient and humorous through trials and tribulations, something I'm proud to inherit and share with others.

All of this insight becomes available when we just accept what is.

Here's another example of acceptance. In my seminars, I often meet women who say things like, "But Loretta, I married an idiot." It sounds funny, but when you feel stuck, it's not so funny. These ladies say, "He won't clean up after himself," or "He won't keep his promises," and on and on. The point is this: Maybe these husbands simply don't have the resources that their wives wished they had. These women can keep working at it and working at it, like a Chihuahua with a bone, but maybe there's just no meat on that particular bone, as it were. Maybe these particular frogs just aren't capable of being the fairy-tale princes their wives want them to be.

What can these women do? I usually suggest that they focus on the things in their lives that they *do* have power over—the way they spend their free time, the way they feel about themselves, their interests and passions, and their other important relationships. These gals have to work on themselves until they get to a point where they can either accept their mates for who they are or feel good about their decision to pack up and move on.

Are there situations in your life that you spend a lot of energy denying the truth about? Where can that get you, ultimately? If you're in a dead-end job, guess what? It is what it is. Why spend years in denial, talking endlessly with co-workers about the incompetent boss, the horrible conditions, or the hope that, sometime soon, a new CEO will arrive and solve all your problems?

Again, I'm not saying that you should just drone on and on in misery. But aren't you better off facing the truth? I hate to tell you this, but you've got a terrible job, which is probably not going to get better unless you do something about it. You might need to have a long talk with your boss about where you see things going for you. Or, you might simply have to find a new job.

Just don't waste another minute of your precious time hoping that divine intervention will change a situation into something it isn't. You need to honor your own strengths, face a difficult truth, and do what you can to improve the situation.

Anti-Anti-Aging

One of the greatest examples of a societal form of denial comes in the form of our culture's obsession with youth. Aging has somehow become a disease. In my most recent pilgrimage to the local bookstore, I was drawn to a section with this big sign: LATEST BOOKS ON ANTI-AGING. My first thought was: *What's this? A section on how to die? Because if I don't age, I die!* But, no, there's too much common sense in that line of thinking.

The latest American fetish is the marketing of books and products that promise to halt or diminish the ravages of getting older. There are pills, potions, and procedures to smooth, tighten, and lift ancient parts that are starting to wind down like an old flabby clock. Ironically, most of the research for these products seems to be done on mice—animals that don't live very long themselves. I personally have never seen a mouse with wrinkles—or a mouse with a facelift for that matter. . . .

As with all new products, the dilemma is how much of what to take and when? Can it *all* be trusted to be safe and effective? Do I take melatonin to sleep better even though it might give me nightmares? Do I take hormones to increase my libido even though I might develop facial hair? (How much sex am I realistically going to have once my husband sees me with a mustache?) How many vitamins do I take, and in what order, and will my body know what to do with them?

80

When I feel concern about aging, I talk to my mother. I can always count on her for some uplifting information: "You think *that's* bad? You haven't seen anything yet!! Wait 'til you hit 90!"

And of course, that makes me feel a whole lot better. Then I see a 60-year-old movie star on TV who says she's never had a nip-and-tuck—no, her perfect face is all natural. Excuse me? How natural is it for her eyebrows to meet her hairline?

Aging has its drawbacks . . . but *not* aging is worse. Spending time and money on looking better is an individual choice. But it's also imperative that we begin to acknowledge and accept that, as we age, we can become spiritual elders to our grandchildren in the process. Showing the generation behind us that we're at constant war with aging sends a lot of inappropriate messages. Many young girls today are so concerned about looking old that they've begun to have surgical procedures that used to be done on 50-year-olds. Believe me, I'm very happy to live in a time where certain parts of our bodies can be reconstructed if that's our heart's desire—in fact, I'd love to start from the ground up. However, one of the most wonderful ways to age is to remove the angry and disappointed look of nonacceptance from our faces. If we replace it with the serenity of acceptance, we'll age with dignity and grace.

81

> *"Of course there is no formula for success, except perhaps an unconditional acceptance of life and what it brings."*
> — Arthur Rubinstein

How Did We Get Here?

Virtually every human being wants more out of life—to be happier, wealthier, more beautiful, smarter, more creative. We're never satisfied with ourselves, and that's probably a good thing. It's what keeps us striving to improve ourselves.

But whoever you are, and whatever you have or don't have, chances are that you've attained a fair amount of self-awareness and happiness by accepting what is. For example, I recently met a woman who grew up in the most dire of straits. Her father was a convicted killer, and her mother—in part out of desperation because of her husband's lot in life—committed suicide. This young woman was the eldest of several children, and she'd had to effectively give up her childhood in order to raise her siblings.

For years, this woman's life and the circumstances that she grew up in were a burden on her psyche. Finally, after doing the hard work of accepting that *it is what it is*—she has not only created a wonderful relationship with her own children, but is also writing a book about her childhood!

82

Take the time to acknowledge and reflect on how and what you've been able to accept throughout your life. Maybe, instead of your millionth pity party, you should have an *acceptance* party! Invite your friends and family members, and give each person a few minutes to share their stories. You'll learn a great deal about them and get some tips for future experiences. Break out the champagne and pass out the party pants . . . you just moved closer to having an amazing life.

❊ ❊ ❊

LAUGH IT UP!

"An amazing life requires humor."

When I was a little girl, I'd often grab a bowler hat and cane so that I could mimic Charlie Chaplin—someone who always made me burst into gales of laughter with his silly gait and twitchy mustache. My entire family loved my portrayal and would egg me on, and the more they laughed, the funnier I became, until I was totally possessed.

Some things never change. Once again, here I am making people laugh to reduce their stress . . . and I love every minute of it. Each time I stand on a stage, I feel blessed to be able to get thousands of people to laugh at themselves. But this wasn't always the case.

When I attended Saint Joseph's Catholic School, the good sisters would call my mother quite often to report my antics. They'd say, "Your daughter is bright but foolish"—ironically enough, I now get paid for it!

Humor became my saving grace. As George E. Vaillant, M. D., of Harvard has said, humor is "man's most elegant coping mechanism." That's certainly true for me—through pain and pleasure, laughter has served me well throughout my life.

When I first became interested in researching the healing effects of humor, there was very little information available. I felt fortunate that a friend told me about Norman Cousins and his pioneering work, *Anatomy of an Illness*. In this book, Cousins described his diagnosis with *ankylosing spondylitis*, a crippling, painful disorder that there was no cure for at the time. He was hospitalized with a fever and paralysis, and traditional medical treatments gave him no relief. So Cousins turned to the theories of Hans Selye, who was among the first scientists to study the effects of stress on physiology. Cousins then deduced that if negative emotions could produce negative chemical changes in the immune system, then why couldn't positive emotions produce positive effects?

He consequently eliminated medications, except for large doses of intravenous vitamin C. He brought in family and friends to watch *Candid Camera* and Marx Brothers and Laurel and Hardy films. The inflammation associated with the disease resolved itself, and Cousins regained his health.

84

In the years since the publication of that book, we've discovered that humor offers us many wonderful benefits—in body, mind, and spirit. I'm always amused by the fact that at last we're beginning to see research that defines the obvious effects of how laughter affects us.

When humor is absent from our lives for long periods of time, we're deemed clinically depressed. We know that laughter provides a buffer between stress and its toxic effects—if we're able to find the humor and laugh at our stress. When we laugh, our heart rate and blood pressure increase, as if we're doing a form of aerobics (Cousins called it "inner jogging"). And we're often relaxed afterwards. The benefits are similar to those of meditation.

The most important thing that I've learned from all this is that laughter has the power to make us kinder to one another. When we're able to laugh together at ourselves, it truly brings us to a higher state of consciousness.

The medical community is starting to catch on, too. Hospitals are using comedy channels and humor rooms to help their patients heal faster and reduce pain (the endorphins released from laughter are natural painkillers). In fact, Columbia-Presbyterian Medical Center in New York City was the first to participate in the "Clown Care Unit," which was founded by

Michael Christensen of the Big Apple Circus. Now, at least 15 hospitals nationwide offer this program, for medical professionals have discovered that when children interact with the clowns, they get better faster. And yet, with all this evidence to support something so obvious, many of us still don't get it.

> *"Humor can be dissected as a frog can, but the*
> *thing dies in the process, and the innards are*
> *discouraging to any but the pure scientist."*
> — E. B. White

86

The Grim Reaper

If we watch people on TV commercials, we're led to believe that we live in a society where people laugh all the time and everybody's always having a great time. The truth is that most of us aren't laughing all that much; in fact, Americans come in at *number 11* in a survey of worldwide humor. But that should come as no surprise—after all, it's pretty hard to crank out those guffaws when we're constantly on the go and all we seem to care about is accomplishing as much as possible. So we don't take the time to appreciate that life is funny—and *we're* the joke! We don't have to spend our days and nights complaining and ruminating about everything that's not going our way. A little humor would really help us relieve our anguish.

EIGHT REASONS
WE CAN'T LIGHTEN UP

1.   **We're too busy.** Let's face it—will we ever
     not be busy? Maybe at our funeral. . . .

2.   **We're afraid of what *they* may say.**
     I don't know who *they* are, but they sure
     stop the laughter for a lot of people.
     (Actually, some of "them" are living
     in my house.)

3.   **The committee is meeting.** Many
     of us are filled with inner critics who
     want us to be terminally serious adults.

4.   **We need to be right.** It's hard to laugh if
     we're always proving a point.

5.   **We have a tendency to judge and criticize.**
     (This comes up a lot, doesn't it?)

6.   **We've got too many rules and regulations.**
     When we behave like drill sergeants and
     life is a forced march, it becomes difficult
     to chuckle.

7.   **We need to suffer** before, during, and
     after anything stressful.

8.   **We've got too much ego.** When we're
     overinflated, we can't laugh because we're
     afraid we'll lose our sense of importance.

87

Our way of life is creating millions of depressed people. There's depression that comes from life's tragedies and depression that stems from biology . . . but a great deal of what we're seeing today is depression that results from people feeling alone and disconnected.

Humor isn't created in a vacuum—it needs people to spread it. Laughter is contagious; our moods affect those around us. I wish every doctor would ask their patients if they're indulging in giant doses of laughter—and also if they're enjoying their lives. Are they socially connected, in good relationships, and getting love and nurturing on a daily basis? *That* would be a wonderful indicator of good mental health.

88

I thank God that we have drugs that are able to help people with mood disorders. But I also believe that some individuals would benefit tremendously from getting a prescription for *laughter:* Have 100 belly laughs and call me in the morning.

Well, it's paying off all around the world. Dr. Madan Kataria, a physician in India, started laughing clubs there to alleviate the stress that many people felt—he now travels the globe with his message. Hundreds of people now meet in parking lots and laugh for half an hour. The hilarity merely starts out as forced "ha-ha-ha's," but it soon spreads like a virus.

Consequently, participants exhibit improved health and decreased feelings of stress.

It's been proven that when we hear someone laugh, we laugh as well. It's an automatic response. Think about being at the movies and missing a joke's punch line, but laughing anyway—then turning to our partner and asking, "What did they say?" We laugh whether we get it or not, and laughter that arises out of pretense elicits the same chemical responses that authentic laughter does.

Shouldn't we be laughing more often?

89

The Four Theories of Humor

There are four major theories about humor, and how and why we human beings find things funny:

1. *The incongruity theory:* This theory says that we laugh when we think we're being led in one direction, only to discover something we didn't expect—a clever twist and a surprise. Larry Dossey, author of *Healing Words: The Power of Prayer and the Practice of Medicine,* calls this "the little ambush of the mind."

2. *The release theory:* This says that we laugh when we're given an outlet to release repressed thoughts—often of a sexual, or sometimes even violent, nature. Most dirty jokes fall into this category. As do a lot of Road Runner cartoons.

3. *The superiority theory:* This theory says that we laugh at other people's misfortune— because it makes us feel better about ourselves. Whenever a child laughs as another kid falls in the playground, that's the superiority theory at work. It's when we laugh *at* someone, not *with* them.

90

4. *The divinity theory:* This says that a lighthearted attitude—the ability to laugh at ourselves and see ourselves as the cosmic joke— can be the most enriching and rewarding of all the styles of humor. This theory of humor is about being able to see our own arrogance and superiority, and laugh at our absurdity. It says that, in fact, spiritual growth can come through humor—by letting us see difficult truths about ourselves, by showing us that the world doesn't revolve around us, and by connecting people—even if only through a shared laugh.

Being in good spirits is the ultimate form of humor. It isn't about being a comedian—we don't have to be Lily Tomlin or Chris Rock to make a positive contribution to the world. It's about recognizing that there is more than *me*—there's a *we* that's also enormously important. It's about helping us see that we're all in this together, so let's make the best of it. Let's be more civil, more empathetic, and a whole lot kinder. For example, I can't tell you how many people I see while traveling who make a huge fuss about the security lines at airports. I'm talking great big self-important hissy fits about how their time is being wasted, how inefficient the system is, and how dare the screeners want to scan them, and on and on. . . .

91

Now, I've got a couple of questions here. First: After September 11, how sane is anybody who makes a fuss about airport security?

Second: So what if it's taking a little long and it's a little inefficient? Of course it is, but these people are doing the best they can in a tough situation.

Third (and most important)—is acting like a three-year-old throwing a tantrum going to make matters any better? You're going to have to be screened; live with it.

When we do things in a playful manner, they become easier and more fun, and we also get so much more cooperation. When I travel and get pulled out of the line, I tell the screeners, "I'm so glad you're screening me. This is the best screening I've had in years!" It usually brings some laughter to the situation. They do what they have to do, life goes on . . . and a little bit of goodwill is left behind for all to share.

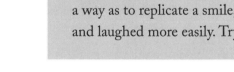

TURN THAT FROWN UPSIDE DOWN

Clark University psychologist James Laird found that when he had participants in a study move their facial muscles in such a way as to create a frown (without calling it that or doing anything else to create a negative attitude), they reported feeling angry. Yet when he had participants move their facial muscles in such a way as to replicate a smile, they felt happier and laughed more easily. Try it yourself!

"A sense of humor is probably
the only divine quality of man."
— Arthur Schopenhauer

Humor As a Coping Mechanism

Whenever I give a lecture or a workshop, I never fail to encourage participants to read *Man's Search for Meaning* by Viktor Frankl. He was a psychiatrist who survived the Nazi concentration camps during World War II and who developed a form of psychotherapy called *Logotherapy* as a result. His book profoundly shows how individuals can survive the most horrific of situations through grace, dignity, and humor.

In the Preface of the book, Gordon Allport writes: "Hunger, humiliation, fear, and deep anger at injustice are rendered tolerable by closely guarded images of beloved persons, by religion, by a grim sense of humor, and even by glimpses of the healing beauties of nature—a tree or a sunset." I've heard many accounts of how this type of humor, called "gallows humor," has helped many people in difficult jobs, particularly health-care professionals. Anyone overhearing some of the conversations between nurses or doctors might be deeply offended, but for them it becomes a way to get relief from the horrors they witness.

As a child, I was dragged to many an Italian funeral, which often resembled a Federico Fellini movie. There was great drama as the black-clad women wailed and moaned. Then there'd be bursts of laughter as people began to recount stories about the dearly departed. And, of course, it would all end with a giant feast. I learned that there's a very short distance between tears and laughter—they both offer relief.

How to Humor Your Life

When I first began teaching, I thought that the best way to get people to laugh was for me to be as funny as possible so they'd giggle nonstop. As I evolved and researched the subject, I realized that although there were benefits to this model, it didn't allow people to be able to laugh at *themselves*. And that was my goal—because when people can get to that point, they always travel with their own comedy act that's ready to lighten up their life.

After years of trying different techniques, I came across Albert Ellis and his work. As I read his book *Rational Emotive Behavior Therapy: A Therapist's Guide*, the words "we disturb ourselves" jumped out at me, and I had an epiphany: We all do this in some manner. We take something relatively easy to cope with and make it into a crisis. Haven't we all been with someone who goes on and on about the fact that "It's raining! What are we going to do? We're going to get wet, and our hair will be a mess," and on and on.

94

This is completely irrational, but these people can't seem to appreciate that. They're more invested in making themselves nuts. They've certainly seen rain and have gotten wet before, and nothing catastrophic happened then . . . so why can't they just grab an umbrella and get over it? But the rain isn't really the issue, is it? I'm convinced that we don't want to stop whining, because in some way it gives us attention. And since most of us aren't feeling very appreciated or nurtured, we use negativity as a way to get our needs met—even though we know that it turns people off.

One of the ways we can begin to shift this behavior and make ourselves and everyone around us feel better is to use the art of exaggeration. It's simply a twist on the way we disturb ourselves. In other words, if you're passionately pursuing guilt, try exaggerating the feeling. Viktor Frankl calls this "paradoxical intention," which in more simplistic terms means that if we intentionally disturb ourselves to the point where we get to an extreme place, it becomes ridiculous. It helps create the ability for self-detachment . . . you become *you looking at you.*

For example, suppose you went out to a fancy dinner and not only ate an entire porterhouse steak and French fries, but a luscious piece of chocolate cake with whipped cream for dessert. Personally, I don't find this cause for self-flagellation, but many people do.

They'll wake up the next day and want to kill themselves. They'll berate themselves for their lack of self-control, feeling guilty and angry for their indulgence, and they'll start doing penance in the form of over-exercising and dieting to the point of near-starvation.

If this sounds like you, here's what I suggest: Really go for it. Don't just run five miles on the treadmill and eat a rice cake for lunch. Fantasize and go nuts! Fully absorb yourself in the intensity of it—give in to your guilt! What's this horrible, despicable indulgence really going to do to you? You ate a steak. God, you're a disgusting creature. You have no self-control whatsoever. And French fries, too. *And* dessert. How can you walk down the street and look people in the eye? Maybe you need to just crawl into bed and never come out; nobody wants to look at you. Besides, by now your clothes probably don't fit, so you can't get dressed and leave the house anyway. And even if you did, people would just snicker as you walked by. You should go ahead and say good-bye to your husband and children, because they'd be better off if they weren't saddled with a pig like you around the house. After all, what kind of role model could you possibly be?

Eating chocolate cake with whipped cream?! Before you know it, the kids are going to be eating chocolate cake and whipped cream, too, and then *their* lives will be over as well. It's better to leave them now, let them fend for themselves, or get them a new mother who won't embarrass them in such a grotesque and humiliating fashion. Let them find a mother who deserves their love—one who only eats organic sprouts and tofu.

And then what? What happens after you pack your bags and kiss the photos of your children good-bye, leaving little whipped-cream marks in the shape of your lips on the picture frames? You can go down-town, get a table at McDonald's, and never leave. Just take all the money out of your bank account and sit there, eating Big Macs and hot apple pies until they have to bring in a crane to pluck you out of the place because you can no longer fit through the doors. They'll have to build a special wing for you at the local zoo, next to the elephant habitat, because there's no human dwelling that can accommodate you. Local children will come by and point, throw peanuts at you, and giggle.

Having fun yet? How about this one: You overslept and are running 15 minutes late for a staff meeting. Your boss is going to be furious. How could you be so stupid?

Take off from there: You're going to walk into the office, and your boss will be standing at the front door, arms crossed, with the rest of the company glaring out from behind him.

"Jones," he'll say, "you missed the meeting."

"I'm sorry," you'll reply.

"Sorry? Did you hear that, people? She's sorry,"

your boss will say, as your co-workers all laugh, stare, and whisper.

"This company has gone out of business, and it's all your fault," your boss will tell you. "This business was started by my grandfather 120 years ago, and in one morning, you destroyed it all."

You'll start to walk away, when someone calls from the back: "I've had to pull my kids out of their school because we can't afford it anymore."

"My wife left me for someone who's employed!" yells another.

You crawl back to your car and go home, but by the time you get there, your family is already gone. All that remains is a note: *How could you shame us this way? I've gone home to Mother and you'll never see your children again.*

You do the math: Without a job, you'll only be able to pay your mortgage for another two months. Of course, no one will ever employ you again after your oversleeping fiasco, so you'll have to sell the house. You're a worthless creature: broke, without a family, living on the street, begging passersby for handouts.

You'll find that the more you're able to take your stresses to their absurd conclusions, the more diffused they'll become. You'll start to see that your obsessions and concerns are probably out of whack with reality. What's really going to happen if you eat a rich dinner? Probably nothing. Maybe you'll put on an ounce or two.

If you do it *every day*, that's another story . . . then you very well could end up in the elephant house.

> *"Humor is just another*
> *defense against the universe."*
> — Mel Brooks

You and Jerry Seinfeld

Another great technique that I use with clients is to help them picture their life as a sitcom. I'll bet that if you tried, you could write a script that takes the things about your friends and family that sometimes drive you crazy (and the things you love, too) yet make them funny. I don't know anybody who doesn't have enough strange people and relationships in their lives to make a comedy that rivals *Seinfeld*.

Think about it: What are some of the quirks of people you know, and how could they be twisted around if that person were a character in a sitcom? My mother, for example, has the ability to push every one of my buttons and drive me absolutely insane. She's never been easy, and now, if anything, her advanced age has made her even more difficult. It's taken off the soft edges and left her feeling that she can say anything. For instance, a few weeks ago, she told me that I'm starting to resemble an egg.

99

Now, that's a funny line. But it sure didn't feel funny to me when she said it (as I was putting on a new dress and was looking at myself in the mirror). It hurt; and it was invasive, disrespectful, and rude. It's one of those things that relatives (*my* relatives, at least) think they can say to *you*, but never to anyone outside the family.

Well, if I think of my mother as a character in a sitcom, somehow it takes the sting away. I envision her played by Estelle Getty, who was the mother on *The Golden Girls*. I see her as a wacky old lady, saying whatever she wants, driving all the people around her crazy. I picture her coming in and out of scenes, saying absurd things to people, and going back to whatever she was doing before. I imagine my husband stoically throwing one-liners at her, staying above the fray like good sitcom husbands usually do (instead of the reality of the situation, which is that I really want him to blast her for me and get furious when he doesn't!).

Got it? Can you write a script for yourself?

Who's the main character? Is there a loyal best friend? An annoying neighbor? The self-centered co-worker? The pitiful sibling? Who's the love interest? Do you have a character who reminds you of George Costanza from *Seinfeld?* Ethel Mertz from *I Love Lucy?* Hot Lips Houlihan from *M*A*S*H?* Is there a know-it-all like Diane from *Cheers?* A ditsy

roommate like Chrissy Snow from *Three's Company?*
A nosy neighbor like Mrs. Kravitz in *Bewitched?*

Do some of the people in your life have funny little quirks that would look hilarious if they were on a
TV screen? Does anyone pick their teeth loudly? Or
start every sentence with the same word? All of these
examples can help you fill out the details of your psychological sitcom and make you see how funny the stuff
around you sometimes is—even the stuff that drives you
the craziest.

> *"A sense of humor is part of the art of leadership,*
> *of getting along with people,*
> *of getting things done."*
> — Dwight D. Eisenhower

101

Faking Good Humor

You know you can do it. No matter how angry and
miserable you are, if the phone rings, you pick it up and
in your most pleasant voice, say "Hello?" And if you
keep up the pretense of pleasantness, when the conversation is over, you'll no longer feel quite as angry.

If you walk around with a scowl on your face, no
one's going to want to make you feel better. But we
human beings tend to mimic one another—which

means that if you walk around with a smile on your face, pleasantly swing your arms, and look like you're having a grand old time, you're going to elicit similar gestures from others. We tune in to the moods and behaviors of others—so if you fake being in good spirits, other people around you will catch on, their mood will lift—and so will yours!

The effect of "good humor" is so much more powerful than even the huge effect on the psyche of a good laugh. I mean, wouldn't it be lovely if, at the end of a concert or a ball game, instead of everyone barreling down the aisles trying to get to their car first, people stayed to chat in the aisles to talk about what they just saw?

I love to talk to people wherever I go—in elevators, in checkout lines, at intersections. When my husband is with me, he always asks the same question: "Why are you talking to those people? You don't even know them." I always give him the same answer: "Well, that's the point, isn't it?" When you talk to someone, you get to know them. I ask people how they're feeling today. I tell them if I like their outfit. I comment on whatever is happening around us.

I often say something funny, but that's because it's my style. The other day at the supermarket, the woman doing the bagging asked me whether I wanted paper or plastic. And I asked her what she thought the advantages were of each. After she explained how some people like paper for environmental reasons, while some liked plastic because it's more flexible and easy to carry, I thought long and hard. Then I told her that it doesn't matter to me—a bag's a bag. In fact, I'm an old bag myself. What's one old bag to another?

She laughed and said, "We don't get too many like you!"

I'm sure she doesn't! But that's not the point. The point is, what I said to that woman made the moment lighter and brought a little kindness and communication into each of our lives.

Keep in mind that laughter is a social lubricant. It's so easy to turn something that's usually irritating into something fun. Next time you're stuck in line somewhere, instead of stewing about it and driving yourself and everyone around you crazy, start talking to the people around you. Say something like, "Well, it's really great being here with all of you. How about ordering some pizza while we're waiting? I've got my TV and VCR here in my handbag. We can pop in a movie and wait it out. . . ."

People might initially look at you in a strange way, but believe me, they'll soon join in . . . they always do. And if you're just not the sort of person who feels comfortable being silly, then just say hello or ask how someone is. It will change the spirit of the moment immeasurably. It's really quite simple to take the little actions that bring good humor into your life. It's often nothing more than a gesture, a greeting, or a funny comment. It's a little moment of communication that might be meaningless—or it just might turn out to be life-changing.

Laughter makes life easier—it allows us to see the absurdity of it all and gives our brains a vacation and a reality check. All in all, being in good humor keeps life simpler, lighter, and more humane.

❋ ❋ ❋

6

Put a Spin on It

"An amazing life requires creativity."

When I conduct my workshops, I often ask people to think about the things that stress them out, and then we re-create them in different ways. I have them sing, dance, and act out their stressors. These exercises are usually very different from anything they're accustomed to doing. And that's the point.

When we put a new spin on things, it helps us gain new perspective, and we often get unstuck. But most of us would rather face a firing squad than do something new and unusual. When faced with the prospect of thinking or acting differently, we tend to revert to saying things like, "I've been doing this for years. This is who I am." If any statement drives me up a wall, it's that one. No! It's *not* who you are— you're so much more.

We should never be content to be thwarted, inhibited versions of ourselves. Since the beginning of time, human beings have desired to be more, make more of ourselves, and essentially go where no one has dared to go before. Inside all of us is a deep desire to be creative. We're born full of curiosity, and we yearn to be unique.

Watch a child as he flies around the house, pounding the coffee table, removing his underpants and gingerly placing them on his head, giggling the whole time at his creative antics. How many of us have been corrected by our parents: "Stop banging on the coffee table! Don't put underpants on your head!"

The child sees everything with "new eyes"—something most of us tend to lose along the path to adulthood. It's safer to "fit in," so we stop experimenting and daring to be silly. That's why it's ironic that many of the people we admire for being bold and different aren't really that unique. It's simply that they've chosen to expand their minds and souls rather than retract them.

This isn't a chapter about how to access your inner artist or ballerina, but rather how to move out of the cardboard box your mind may inhabit so you can move into glorious places filled with colors, shapes, and unique people; and brilliant, shiny, thoughts. I get excited just writing about the possibilities of who and what we can become. . . .

Look in the Mirror

Every day we wake up and perform our rituals, many of which are quite satisfying. I rather enjoy sitting in my cozy chair, drinking my cup of coffee while I gaze out the window at my garden. Even though I've heard that standing on my head is healthy and brings blood flow to my brain, it's not something I'd prefer to be doing first thing in the morning. That really wouldn't help me get a new spin on things . . . it would just make me dizzy.

Our rituals can be good for us, and they can be comforting, too (I certainly have no intention of giving up my morning coffee in my cozy chair). But an unyielding reliance on ritual can be destructive—not only to ourselves, but to society as well.

107

When we become inflexible, we start to feel as if we're living our own version of the movie *Groundhog Day*—the same thing, day in and day out. And that sort of inflexibility in ritual and thought, in its most extreme form, leads to cultish behavior.

It's exciting to realize that some of the latest brain research shows that if we develop new ways of thinking and being, we may actually be able to stave off the effects of dementia. If we stop spending so much time on our exterior world and spend more time on our interior world, there's no end to the good it would do us. People are always talking about going to the gym and doing their "workout," but shouldn't we be giving our minds a workout, too? How about a *mind* gym?

In his book *Aging with Grace,* Dr. David Snowden shares his studies on a group of nuns he's been tracking for a number of years. Many of them live well into their 90s, and a surprising number of them are 100 years of age. They also suffer fewer and milder forms of dementia, Alzheimer's disease, and brain afflictions than other people. Snowden found that the sisters challenge themselves with crossword puzzles, vocabulary quizzes, and debates; hold current-events seminars, and write in their journals. Snowden, who examined more than 100 brains donated at death by The School Sisters of Notre Dame, maintains that axions and dendrites that usually shrink with age branch out and make new connections if they receive enough intellectual stimulation. The old adage "Use it or lose it" really applies here.

What Stops the Spinning?

There are many reasons why we become trapped in our routines. The obvious one is that creativity is losing ground in the quagmire of mass marketing. Every single day, we're bombarded with images that reflect what we should be wearing, using, doing, or thinking about. The latest form of group insanity is yoga. Over the years, I've seen fitness fads come and go, but I never thought that yoga would become so mainstream. Wrong! Several months ago, *Time* magazine had model Christy Turlington on the cover in a yoga pose—since then, all things yoga have surfaced. We eventually may be known as "Yoga Nation," as there is now couples' yoga, senior citizens' yoga, kids' yoga, and soon, I'm sure, we'll see dog and parrot yoga. There are yoga mats, cushions, candles, magazines, books, videos. . . .

I'm not at odds with the fact that people are more in tune with the concept; it's what's *behind* it that's disturbing. As a culture, we seem to have to do what everyone else is doing, rather than examining our own creative instincts. It could be that twisting into a pretzel while we're chanting just might make us anxious— we might be better off swimming, fencing, or learning how to tango. But no, we defer to what we consider to be the "thing" of the moment.

How far we've strayed from following our inner muse. Can you imagine trying to get a group of two- or three-year-olds to all do the same thing? It would be like trying to reign in a bunch of wild stallions. Lives of bland uniformity lead us away from a life of joy and celebration. We need to cross boundaries and stand out from the crowd if we're going to put our own spin on it.

The File Pile

The organizational police are taking over this country. Bookstores sell hundreds of books that try to persuade us to train ourselves to get rid of things we don't need; and show us how to take what we *do* need and hang it; fold it; color-coordinate it; or put it into a tube, container, or shelf. Of course, don't forget that we also have to feng shui everything—which means that our furniture has to face the right direction, otherwise all our relationships and business deals will go down the toilet. . . .

110

I'm probably the Antichrist of organization. I don't have an organizer or Palm Pilot, and this drives my friends nuts. I continually get asked, "How do you remember appointments and phone numbers?" It's simple: I do it the way everybody on the planet did it before those damn things came out—I commit the information to memory, so my brain becomes my internal organizer. My mother managed to get through life and have an amazing career on Wall Street (working for a very prominent law firm) without an organizer.

My father owned a huge bakery in Brooklyn with many employees. No organizer.

I know that the disciples of organization reading this are ready to burst because they're dying to tell me what I'm missing and how I could do so much more if I had the *Bible of Doing* under my arm. Maybe that's the point. Once we're carrying around something that has every moment of the day accounted for, without any time out for playfulness and spontaneity, we once again become slaves to conformity . . . and conformity dulls the mind.

Now, I'm sure that organizers are helpful in some ways, but they're also destructive. Reliance on them to the exclusion of exercising our memory begins to deteriorate our ability to remember. Our brain adapts to its workload, and having a good memory is critical to creativity. It helps us make connections that can give birth to new concepts and ways of being.

These days, scientists seem to believe that true genius is often the product of a somewhat unstructured, chaotic mind. Great inventors and artists often seem to share a randomness of interests and passions. They're not structured—they seem to fall into one thing as easily as another, as if their interests are like boats upon the waves. They often find their way to greatness by anything but careful advance planning— in fact, it often feels like pure happenstance. They're engaged by everything that life has to offer, and they happily and messily move from one thing to the next,

111

quenching their thirst for excitement, knowledge, and entertainment.

Perhaps our reliance on structure and organization hurts our ability to think outside the lines. . . .

Dress to Express

When's the last time you saw someone dressed flamboyantly? Well, I just spent two weeks in Province-town, Massachusetts, and I can honestly say that I was blown away by the fabulous combinations of clothing I witnessed daily. Whimsy was prevalent everywhere. I saw one outrageous outfit after another, and people sauntered down the street looking delighted with themselves. No one was trying to prove anything—they were just creatively comfortable.

It was such a relief to see folks dressed in whatever they wanted—and not what the magazines were saying is the "in" thing this season. It's good to stretch the imagination a little when you dress. Wear a hat once in a while; buy a boa; choose a color you love but are afraid to wear because the fashion FBI say it's "out" this year. Pretend you're back to playing dress-up. Or have a few friends over and ask them to wear something they'd never dare wear in public. You might have always

112

dreamed of looking like a rock star, or maybe you're more the Cinderella type. . . .

Don't wait until Halloween! You can put on a costume any old day.

The World Around You Is Spinning

Creativity is all around you—all you have to do is be awake to it.

In this often too-busy world, it's easy to become deadened to the unique and different. Yet the universe is constantly creating and re-creating itself: Stars die and new ones emerge; the wind is soft and caressing, or it's fierce and relentless; clouds form into a myriad of patterns. When was the last time you looked up into the sky and saw a cartoon character or an animal in the clouds?

113

Many people wake up each day and immediately turn on the TV so they can see what's happening in the world. Now, I'm all for being informed, but having some quiet mornings now and then could leave you open to more inner peace. After all, a quiet mind becomes more creative. I realize that many of you have kids, pets, and a whole host of distractions that don't allow for much quiet time. But turning off the

TV will lessen the chaos. Play some classical music instead, or have your kids tell jokes while they're having breakfast. I'll even go so far as to suggest that you read them some poetry. The point is that there are many creative solutions that can fit into your life in many different ways.

I know the head of a big New York City advertising agency who probably earns well over a million dollars a year. His peers, and even some of the people who work for him in executive positions, are picked up by a car and driver and shuttled around town in high

style. But this man rides a bicycle to the office every day. It's got nothing to do with the cost; the money is meaningless to him. Riding a bike makes him feel young, vibrant, and fit; and it puts him closer to the excitement of the city. It makes him feel sharp and in control, while riding in the back of a car makes him feel lethargic and idle.

Of course, my friend is perceived as being crazy and eccentric for doing this. The people he associates with all think that they've earned the right to be driven around in a company car; it's a symbol of their importance and status. They're at the top of their fields, and they want everyone to know it. And, of course, their beautiful suits never get splashed by a taxi speeding through a puddle, as happens regularly to the man on the bike. It would be a whole lot easier for this executive to allow himself to be driven to work; it's more lavish, leisurely, and elegant; and people would stop thinking of him as a weirdo. So why doesn't he do it?

Because he honors himself. He knows what he prefers, and he doesn't really care what other people think. He feels self-confident enough so that the symbolism of the high-status car and driver don't hold any appeal for him. By choosing to do things his own way and not buying in to the "norm," he feels much more like his own man.

You're Too Much

We're often critical and judgmental about people's looks, personalities, or ways of thinking. I was always attacked for being too sensitive: "You should toughen up, Loretta. You're too nice." Well, that's all well and good, but my sensitivity to others has been one of the reasons I'm successful in my career. Of course, it does have its downfalls. Many times, being overly sensitive feels as if I'm a walking satellite dish, picking up everybody's stuff and transmitting it back to myself. But without sensitivity, a major portion of art, music, and poetry would not exist.

We spend many hours of our lives pointing out what we think should be adjusted so that it fits some kind of picture that we have in our minds. We berate ourselves with what we think we should be: We should be tougher or smarter; or more aggressive, sensitive, or innovative. But if we try to embrace—not erase—what we're seeing, hearing, and feeling, we may learn something new, or connect to something that could increase our ability to be more joyful. It may also jog our own inner creator.

THE DEATH OF CREATIVITY COMES FROM:

✳ Sticking with what works
✳ Fear and stress
✳ Being a control freak
✳ Having a critical nature
✳ Always seeing what's there versus what's not there
✳ Being too logical, not playful
✳ Too many *don'ts*

How to Get to Eureka

Creative episodes are most productive when preceded by meditation or some form of aerobic exertion.

So take a few minutes, settle down into your favorite chair, and try this out:

Take a few nice deep breaths and let them out slowly. Start at your feet—squeeze your toes and then release them; tighten your calves and upper thighs, then gently let them go. Make fists and then release them; tighten your arms, and let them go. Tighten your abdomen, your back, and your shoulders, and gently let them go (yes, you can let your stomach hang out!). Tighten your face, and let it go. Take another couple of breaths, and let your whole body sink into the chair.

117

Now imagine yourself in a beautiful field of magnificent flowers. You're very excited to be in the midst of the heady fragrance and profusion of colors. You've come with a large basket so that you can pick and choose the ones you want and bring them back home. As you bend over to smell one of the flowers, you notice that in the center of it is written a word. It says SING.

As you meander through the field, you notice that the center of every flower contains a word: WRITE, PAINT, DANCE, INSPIRE, JUMP, SPIN, PLAY. You're finding yourself dazed by all the beauty and all the choices, but you pick and

*pick until your basket is full. Your entire spirit
is renewed, and your mind is filled with all the
wonderful ideas that the flowers inspired in
you. Now see yourself gently returning to being
present in your cozy chair. Yawn and stretch
like a cat, keeping with you the memory of
the wonderful bouquet of creative ideas you
brought back.*

*Make sure to keep some flowers in a vase
somewhere to remind you that you're capable of
many creative moments.*

118

Dance to Find a New Spin

As I mentioned earlier, in my workshops I have
people do interpretive dances to illustrate the stressors
in their lives. Can you imagine the incredible fun we
have when people, many of whom may not have moved
their bodies in creative ways for years, now have to
marry the concept of stress and dance? Gabrielle Roth,
a famous dance therapist, speaks about this technique
in her book, *Sweat Your Prayers*. She says that a lot of
stress has a staccato feel to it—if we took the time to
dance it, we could release the tension.

One woman in my workshop spent a great deal of
time discussing her inability to stop worrying. She

actually raised the level to new heights by worrying about her constant worrying. By our final day together, after we'd gone through several different ideas and techniques, she was feeling that *nothing* could help her.

I then divided the group into ten teams of five people each. I told them that they needed to choose one group member's stressor to create a dance around. I'd brought a wonderful array of music with me that featured a lot of drumming and rhythm. I told the participants to wear one of my costumes (of which I have many) or arrange their own clothing in an unusual way. I gave them 15 minutes to plan the presentation, because too much time makes people start thinking too much.

I heard all kinds of excuses: "I have two left feet," "This feels strange," "I can't do this" . . . all of which I ignored. We all love to come up with excuses why we "can't" do something, don't we? The *can'ts* always seem to far outweigh the *cans*. So I insisted that these people show me what they *can* do.

Time was up, and the show started. Each group was amazing. An accountant who had felt taken advantage of at work was dressed by her team in a black cloak. They put her in the center of the circle and danced around her moaning, "Poor thing, poor, poor thing," like a Greek chorus. We absolutely could not control ourselves. The laughter was endless . . . but even more

119

important, the technique finally helped the belea-
guered accountant recognize her martyrdom.

The most amazing dance came from my friend the
worrier and her group. They started in the corner and
deliberately and slowly showed the feelings of worry.
With furrowed brow, their hands on their temples
feigning despair, they hunched over and looked at each
other with startled expressions. I was truly in awe; it was
a powerful experience for all of us. In movement, they
managed to effectively demonstrate the pain and
destructiveness of worry.

But even more profound was the way this creative
exercise changed the woman's perception of how and
what she worried about. I saw her almost six months
later, and she said it literally changed her thinking.
She now saw her own role in continuing the "dance"
of worry, and the terrible effects it had on her life.
That recognition helped her gain control over her
obsessive behavior.

None of these people are going to end up performing with Alvin Ailey—that's not the point. They
didn't need to create something lasting, or even something particularly hip. They simply needed to *create*—
to use the process as a path to release stress and see a
new way to think about a problem.

Stuck Between Floors

We rarely use our creative juices to think of different ways to look at everyday items or situations. For instance, every once in a while, you might be on an elevator and find yourself thinking, *What if I got stuck in here? What would I do?* Well, here's your chance: The next time you have a few friends over, instead of playing the same old parlor games, try a brainstorming session.

Sit in a circle and appoint someone the secretary. He or she will record the ideas, but will also participate. Set a timer for 15 minutes. The point of brainstorming isn't to be ponderous—it's to say whatever comes up—good, bad, or indifferent. And fast.

121

Now here's the assignment. You're in an elevator with five other people when the elevator suddenly stops. You're between floors, the lights are out, and the air conditioner has quit. Try to think of at least 100 ways you could amuse yourself while you're stuck. There will be a lot of moans about the number (which always fascinates me, because there's no end to the creative ways we can make ourselves upset). Allow everyone to express themselves without any criticism from anyone else. Whenever you hear a great idea, jump on board and add to it.

Ready, set, go! Here are some starters:

- ❋ Group hugs
- ❋ Individual massages
- ❋ A meditation group
- ❋ A new choir group called "The Elevator Shafts"
- ❋ Graffiti in the dark (and when the lights come back on—surprise!)
- ❋ Foreign language classes
- ❋ Sex
- ❋ Therapy sessions
- ❋ Poetry readings
- ❋ Playing *Survivor* (and voting someone off the elevator)

Keep going. . . .

CUT AND PASTE
YOUR WAY TO GOOD HEALTH

Collaging is another way to release creative energy and use an artistic endeavor to get in touch with emotions. I have people sit with stacks of magazines and big sheets of poster paper, and I ask them to cut and paste illustrations, photographs, or even headlines that express something about their lives—including their hopes, dreams, and disappointments.

Sometimes I have people make two different collages: one to illustrate their lives the way they are now; one to illustrate the life they wish they had. The power of that exercise is often startling. One woman I worked with did a collage of her life now that was, in fact, full of lovely pictures of homes and gardens, nature, and art. She then did a collage of the life she wanted and, at first glance, it wasn't all that different: a lot of nature, interiors, some coastal scenes. She looked at the two and couldn't even see the difference. I asked her why she'd chosen to put some clippings on one poster versus the other, and she honestly didn't know why some felt more like the life she wanted than the life she had.

But I saw it instantly. The collage for the present life was lovely, but all the colors were muted and quiet: browns, greens, earth colors. The collage for the life she wanted had illustrations with the same sort of content, but a very different color palette: bold, vibrant reds, purples, yellows, and oranges. When I pointed that out to her, she gasped out loud. She wasn't able to see the lack of boldness in her own life, for she had buried her inner muse deep within her. But by using her own free-form creativity, this exercise brought it out of her effortlessly.

*"I am certain of nothing but of the holiness of the
heart's affections and the truth of imagination."*
— John Keats

Dare to Be Different

Many of us think that creativity only comes from
individuals who are predisposed to be artistic, musical, or inventive (or other characteristics we've been
taught are acceptable creative endeavors). But I hope
this chapter has shattered a few myths you might have
had about the process. I encourage you to continue
your own journey toward a more creative life. Read
*Creativity: Flow and the Psychology of Discovery and
Invention* by Mihaly Csikszentmihalyi. He recom-
mends that you try to be surprised every day, that you
start doing more of the things that you love and less
of the things you hate, and that you find a way to
express those things that move you.

Every one of us needs to put our own unique spin
on things. Do so boldly and with great joy.

TOO MUCH OF A
GOOD THING
CAN BE TOO MUCH

"An amazing life requires moderation."

When I was a young girl, my mother would respond to my mischievous ways by saying, "You're just too much." I've since come to recognize that this behavioral description can either be a cure or a curse.

We live in a time of great abundance, yet many of our minds are spiritually empty. There was a time when we behaved with more humility and respect because we weren't caught up in thinking that we were the center of the universe. Then came the Self-Esteem Train, and everyone got on board. The thinking was that if we didn't think highly enough of ourselves, we'd be unsuccessful and unfulfilled. However, after spoon-feeding a few generations of kids with the self-esteem elixir, we're now seeing that instead of becoming full of joy and success, they simply became full of *themselves*.

In the October 8, 2002, edition of *Time* magazine, Andrew Sullivan described this phenomenon:

> New research has found that self-esteem can be just as high among D-students, drunk drivers, and former Presidents from Arkansas as it is among Nobel laureates, nuns, and New York City firefighters. In fact, according to research preformed by Brad Bushman of Iowa State University and Roy Baumeister of Case Western Reserve University, people with high self-esteem can engage in far more antisocial behavior than those with low self-worth. "I think we had a great deal of optimism that high self-esteem would cause all sorts of positive consequences and that if we raised self-esteem, people would do better in life," Baumiester told the *New York Times*. "Mostly, the data have not borne out." Racists, street thugs, and school bullies all polled high on the self-esteem charts. And you can see why. If you think you're God's gift, you're particularly offended if other people don't treat you that way.

There was a time when effort was its own reward. Not today. No matter what's going on, somebody thinks they deserve a prize for it. Children who consistently miss the ball are given the same accolades as a team member who hits home runs. I'm not saying that kids should be made to feel inadequate when they don't have the skills to be the best, but neither should they be deluded into thinking that they're going to get into the Hall of Fame if they don't even know how to hold a bat.

I think *we're* batty for fostering this behavior. It simply allows for a sense of deservingness that's unsubstantiated by performance. It prolongs narcissistic behavior and a sense of entitlement, which should decrease as children grow, not increase.

127

This is probably the primary reason we've all gotten into a "More is better" type of existence.

Popcorn, French Fries, and a Coke

Have you been to the movies lately? Can you please tell me what's going on with the size of the snacks? If you want some popcorn to munch on during the film, you get a tub that could feed a family of seven. It looks like something I used to carry out into the yard to rake up leaves.

And the Coke could be a swimming pool for a small child. A large soda in a movie theater is now a 24-ounce vat of pop. Twenty-four ounces! If you ask me, the only person who should be having 24 ounces of liquid is someone who's about to get a sonogram!

The Culture of Excess

The size of movie snacks is just one little symbol of something that's become epidemic in this country. We believe that more is better in everything we do, buy, eat, and see. We take everything to extremes—and how good can that be for our mental and physical well-being?

It's no secret that Americans eat too much, but we also eat too much of the wrong things. Why in God's name does anyone need a "super-sized" portion of French fries? What's *that* all about? We eat enormous portions of fast food and junk food, and even those of us who try to eat moderately tend to consume way too much protein and fat when measured against what's common in other, healthier cultures around the world. But we just can't stop.

128

I recently read that the average American snacks every 45 minutes. I burst out laughing when I read that—I mean, who's out there gathering this information? And how do they do it? Has anyone ever come up to you while you're standing around munching on potato chips and casually inquired, "So, how long has it been since your last snack?" The real response should be, "Since I last recognized that I don't get enough nurturing, such as hugs, loving touches, or kind comments." Isn't that why we stuff our faces—because our hearts and souls aren't being filled up?

I'm not trying to lay a guilt trip on anybody, but do we really need to be eating every 45 minutes? We've become a nation of grazers, always looking for the next feeding station.

129

In our society, work used to be a part of our lives. We'd go to work, we'd come home, and we'd have time off. No more. These days, if we're not on the job 24/7, we're called a slacker! We need to be available by cell phone and e-mail at all hours, 365 days a year. In fact, why don't we just walk around with one of those intravenous bags at our side and have our e-mail messages drip right into our veins?

Time off? Who gets that anymore? Nobody in America, it seems. The average number of vacation days taken by Italians each year is 47; for Germans, 36. Americans average about 11. And even when we do take vacations, they tend to become another job. Every minute is filled with scheduled activity, and now a simple stay on a Caribbean beach is beefed up to become an experience for *National Geographic*. This means going by helicopter to an active volcano, being dropped near the rim with bread and water, and being checked on in five days to see if we've turned into toast.

130

We've all heard this funny comment, attributed to an executive at a big Hollywood studio: "If you don't come in to work on Saturday, don't bother coming in on Sunday." When we stop to think about the impact of anxiety and pressure on other areas of an employee's life and family, is that really funny?

TMI (Too Much Information)

We have to know everything that's going on in the world. *Everything.* At all times. Twenty-four hours a day, we need to have immediate access to every bit of information about what's going on, and we need to be able to find it out in 20 seconds or less. We can't just turn on the Golf Channel to find out what's happening in the sport—no, that's not enough. God forbid we might have to sit there and actually *listen* to the sportscasters and watch the sport. No, we have to look at the scroll running across the bottom of the screen telling us everything *else* that's happening, too—everything that he's *not* talking about.

> *"Minds, like bodies, will often fall*
> *into a pimpled, ill-conditioned state*
> *from mere excess of comfort."*
> — Charles Dickens

It's not enough for us to go see a movie and either like it or not like it. We have to know its standings at the box office that weekend, and whether or not there's been a "drop-off" from the week before. We need to know how much money the film cost to make, whether the director went over budget (and if so, by how much), and how long it's going to take for the studio to recoup its investment—including overseas distribution. We need to know all the behind-the-scenes gossip about the stars—where and what they eat, how they stay so trim, where they get their hair done, what designer clothes they buy, what books they read, what church they attend, what their political views are, who they're sleeping with, and what they do together in the bedroom.

And speaking of the bedroom . . . remember when sex was a fairly simple subject? You had certain body parts—and you pretty much knew what to do with them. If you didn't, you figured it out fairly quickly. In fact, wasn't figuring it out with someone you love most of the fun?

Nowadays, just about every single stinking magazine on the newsstand is filled with articles about sexual technique! Not only that, but there are scores of books in the marketplace about how to have mind-blowing sex, amazing sex, death-defying sex, and rocket-powered sex. We have instruction manuals on how to have multiple orgasms, one-hour orgasms, and orgasms that will last until your next birthday and blow out the candles on the cake. In fact, I've seen vibrators that look like Harleys with sidecars.

132

*"Make everything
as simple as possible, but not simpler."*
— Albert Einstein

Going out to dinner used to be a rather simple experience. But these days, many restaurants are presenting what amounts to a theatrical event. The server makes his grand entrance from stage right, announcing, "Good evening. My name is Rasputin, and I'll be your server."

I can't help but counter with, "My name is Loretta, and I'm your customer." My response triggers a stony stare because I've tried to interject a bit of levity into what's clearly a very serious epic drama.

Rasputin then begins his dialogue: "In addition to what's on the menu, we have some specials I'd like to tell you about. Tonight we have hand-washed lettuce from the banks of the Yangtze River, gathered by 100 crones from the Forbidden City and flown in on Bill Gates's private jet. It's topped with bits of wild yak, which was hand-fed by a cult of monks who worship the yak and believe it was responsible for the Big Bang. Topping the dish is a sprinkling of special rice, every kernel of which has been individually polished by a roving troupe of desert nomads. Dessert is a mound of figs found in King Tut's tomb—and each fig contains a special secret of the universe just for you. Are there any questions about the specials?"

133

I'm dying inside at that moment to shout, "Yes, yes! Where are the franks and beans?"

Have we completely lost our minds? How can we possibly live a life of joy and celebration when everything around us is so out of balance? How can we find peace and serenity in our lives when we're being assaulted with data overload and excessiveness at every moment?

So many people I see in my workshops have lost sight of the things they hold near and dear because they've become somewhat anonymous. They feel lost amid all the clutter in their lives. Their days are spent running around, depositing and picking up children from their extensive activities. Meals are eaten quickly, and family time is often spent apart as each member does his own thing.

We shop 'til we drop, gathering more things to surround ourselves with until they consume us instead of the other way around. My friend Myra said that we should outlive our stuff, not have our stuff outlive us. How many of us have ever just sat with a pen in hand and made a *list* of all of our stuff? Most of us wait until we make out our wills, but I believe that thinking about it periodically might give us some insight as to just how excessive we are. For example, I recently went into my closet to grab a pair of black pants and a black top . . . and realized that I have enough black outfits to be the next Johnny Cash!

We All Want the Good Life

Every one of us aspires to a good life. No one wakes up and says, "Please, God, I'm dying to live in a hovel with no electricity or running water." We all

134

want to have a nice home in a decent neighborhood, a reliable car, and the best education for our children. I truly do not believe that we *want* to be mindless consumers, yet it's becoming increasingly difficult to resist the seduction that's all around us. Advertisements are placed everywhere—who would have thought that before you watched a movie, you'd have to sit through at least five commercials? And while you're innocently trying to watch a tennis match, conveniently placed billboards distract you with ads for shoes, TV shows, and various Websites.

Kids are told over and over to get the latest and the greatest, and it becomes a relentless testing of parents' willpower. It's hard to say no when all the other kids have something. But that's where moderation comes in. If you don't say no to them, when will you? Giving in just because other kids were able to torture their parents into saying yes isn't good enough. Perhaps it's time to gather your family and spend a few hours discussing your values—and moderation needs to be one of them. Corporations spend hours writing mission statements; as individuals and families, we need them, too.

135

❉

TURN DOWN THE VOLUME

Life these days is just too darned *loud*. Do we really need to have the sound of a 747 taking off right over our heads re-created in perfect detail whenever we go to the movies?

Restaurants are overwhelmingly noisy: Patrons are yelling, loud music is piped in, and you have to scream to tell the server what you want to eat. "I'll have the split pea soup, please." "What? Who split up?"

136

What are kids thinking who are riding in cars with closed windows, pumping up the volume so high that the street vibrates? The answer is . . . they're not thinking. They've lost their minds, and pretty soon, their hearing will be next. That's a rather steep price to pay for excessive noise.

Studies have proven that loud noise creates tension in the brain; it keeps the brain constantly engaged and distracted, and makes it harder to actually think and concentrate. The brain is more engaged and creative in a quiet space—because it isn't constantly reacting to outside stimuli.

So, take a quiet walk, or sit somewhere peaceful and read. Take some time to just let your mind feel the natural state of uninterrupted peace.

It's critical that we learn moderation—but it's one of the hardest things to get a handle on, isn't it? It's a precarious balancing act, and how can acrobats be taught to stay on the high wire? They can't—they have to get up there and feel the balance for themselves.

I like the extremes of life, especially those that allow me to go beyond my normal comfort zones. Whenever I have to teach something new, I'm anxious, but I'm also excited by the possibility of becoming the "too much" my mother used to call me. However, I realize that I need to pay close attention to the places where I go over the edge—in all ways. It's immoderate to eat six huge meals in a day, but it's also not reasonable to think that the only way to find health, peace, and harmony is to eat nothing but bean sprouts grown on an organic farm in Canada.

137

We need to trust our intuition. We all have an inner wisdom that speaks the truth to us. When we overindulge in food, alcohol, sex, or even watching too much violent entertainment, our body/mind and spirit begin to give us signals. We begin to feel an unease, a dissociation from friends and loved ones and ourselves.

Think about what you're striving for, and whether it's in sync with your value system. When you don't honor who you are or what you stand for, you'll begin to live the life of a hypocrite. Is sex an act of intimacy and fun for you and your partner, or are you straining to mimic what *Cosmopolitan* tells you is the hottest thing? Do you work hard because you want to provide yourself with a good life, or are you trying to outdo your neighbors?

Don't indulge yourself, but don't deny yourself either. It's unhealthy to eat mounds of lasagna every day, but it's just as unhealthy to want it and never allow yourself the pleasure of having some. One of my favorite lines is: *"Just have some lasagna and shut up!"* What kind of life can you have if you're always denying yourself the things you love? Don't give in to obsession, in either direction.

138

Finding the right balance can be a lifelong journey—but it's one that needs to be taken. Each time you ask yourself if you're balanced, it gives you an opportunity to pause and reflect. It allows you to be conscious about the decisions you're making instead of blindly following the herd off a cliff.

In the end, you'll be able to celebrate your life more often, because you will have told your inner two-year-old, "No, you can't have it. You've already had too much."

8

JUST SHOW UP

"An amazing life requires responsibility."

About 15 years ago, my oldest son, John, was starting a landscaping business. We were talking about the new venture, and he was trying to come up with some kind of catchy slogan to put on the side of his truck. He went back and forth with several different plays on words about gardens and the like.

Then I suggested, "How about 'I Show Up!'?" It started out as a kind of a joke—for I personally found it incredibly frustrating when I had an appointment with some sort of service company and they kept me waiting—sometimes for hours, and often they didn't show up at all. What's wrong with coming right out and saying, "I Show Up"? It's like saying, "You can count on me! I'm dependable."

So there it went, right on the side of my son's truck, in big, bold letters. His business is now quite successful.

Don't you wish that everybody in your life came with a slogan around their neck that said the same thing?

"Eighty percent of
success [in life] is showing up."
— Woody Allen

140

In our pursuit of a life full of joy and celebration, simply being responsible and accountable to the people around us is crucial. We're not in this alone—yet more and more we tend to act as if we're not only the captain of the ship, we're the owner and the sole passenger as well. So often, we don't show up—in fact, we go to enormous lengths to show that we're much too busy to show up.

Our society is increasingly full of broken promises, isn't it? I mean, who has time to keep promises anymore? We're all so distracted and stressed out that we never know from day to day what our schedule's going to be like and how full our in-box is going to be—so we run around acting as if we're just victims of our own itineraries. Hey, it's not our fault if we can't take the kids to the movies on Saturday—they'll just have to understand.

We tell our spouses that we'll be home in time for dinner, but at the last minute, that important phone call comes, and we just can't get away. Or we tell a client that no matter what happens, they'll have that report on their desk by Monday . . . even when we know we can't possibly get it there until Wednesday.

Even the larger promises of our society are breakable. Marriages that promise "'Til death do us part," break up within two years. Families split up and three-year-olds who've been told that "I'll never leave you," suddenly find themselves living 200 miles away from their dads or moms. Advertising makes us promises every minute of every day, and we know how dependable those promises are. Politicians who we used to believe would put their lives on the line to protect the American way of life, now answer to popularity polls—they switch their opinions and abandon their promises at the drop of a hat.

Our society no longer seems to honor *dependability*. Even the word seems a little quaint, doesn't it? But what in the world is more important to a happy and joyous relationship than dependability? I think that knowing someone will simply "be there" is probably the most important aspect of any real, close human connection. What good is it to have a relationship with people who are wonderful, engaging, beautiful, and exciting if they're never going to be around when you need them?

"Being there"—just showing up—sounds so simple. But think of all the ways in which what sounds easy can be difficult:

❋ How often do you break appointments with someone you love?

❋ How often do you say you'll finish a task, and then take an extra day or two?

❋ How often do you show up more than five minutes late for an appointment?

❋ How often do you make promises that you know you can't keep?

142

Most of us back out of little pledges and pacts like this every single day. It's not that we try to be unreliable—and we probably do show up for the "big" things. But we need to stay conscious of the fact that every time we do go back on our word, we're chipping away at the foundation of a good relationship.

Deep, joyful human connection grows out of trust and dependability. When you let people down, even in what seems like the smallest of ways, you tear holes in the seal of the friendship.

I think again of the story Michael the taxi driver told me—about how when he was six years old, his father promised him that he'd come back and take the boy to a Patriots game, and he never did. That broken promise colored Michael's entire life.

We have to be so very careful about keeping our promises.

RSVP!

I'm always astounded at how many people don't even have the courtesy to respond when they're *invited* to show up somewhere! How often, particularly in business, do we not return phone calls or RSVP to invitations? Think of the signal that sends: "Not only am I not going to do what you'd like me to do, I don't even think you're worth the time it takes for me to respond. I don't care if you wait around forever, wondering if I might show up."

It's the ultimate in narcissism, isn't it? It's rude, isolating, and demeaning to other people. But it's almost common practice these days.

Everyday courtesies developed as a way for people to show one another that they took responsibility and accountability for their role in the community, that they accepted the rules our culture lives by.

143

I just heard about a book that's full of thank-you notes for people to copy and send to one another. In case it's too hard for you to think of using your own words to thank someone for a gift or a nice gesture, you can simply plagiarize one from this book. What a time-saver!

Isn't that ridiculous? I mean, how much time does it take to say thank you in your own words? But more important, what's the point of a personal gesture if it's totally <u>imper</u>sonal? The person on the receiving end can't possibly feel that the act was sincere and heartfelt—how can a prepackaged sentiment elicit any real emotion? And what sort of psychological message does it send the person on the giving end?

144

Keep 'em Waiting

There's something so horribly arrogant about being late, isn't there? Here's the signal it sends to the other person: "Your time isn't as important as mine," and "I have the power to keep you waiting, so I'll use it."

Everyone has to suffer through the indignity of being kept waiting now and then. But do we ever really focus on what an indignity it is, and how repeatedly keeping someone waiting can ruin a strong relationship?

Why is it so difficult for us to show people that we care about them by showing up when we say we will? We cut corners with our time, only leaving ourselves the bare minimum to get from one place to the next, and, consequently, we're stuck having to break our promises when there's a five-minute traffic delay.

My advice is: Respect others by scheduling in enough time to make sure you arrive promptly.

145

FLEX THAT TIME!

Why is that we never make time in our organizers for "free time," "family time," or "emergency relationship time"? We feel comfortable committing every moment of our lives—and then we get stuck. I think every day should have some cushion time scheduled in so that you can care for the people you need to and make sure you have the flexibility to keep your promises.

❋

Fake It to Make It!

Once again, science has discovered something that common sense has been telling us for years: When we act as if something is true, emotionally it starts to become true. Recent research has determined that if we walk around with a forced smile long enough, we'll ultimately find ourselves cheering up. If we force ourselves to walk with long strides, swinging our arms and holding our head up high with a big smile on our face, we'll feel more powerful and engaged in life than if we shuffle along, dragging our feet, dangling our arms like a gorilla, and staring at the ground.

146

In other words, *creating* the motion *triggers* the emotion.

Doesn't that make sense? We all know that when we're not feeling great, if we cancel our plans and sit home and linger in our misery, we feel worse. If we push ourselves through the discomfort, get dressed, and go out to the dinner party anyway, we may feel a bit uneasy at the beginning, but before long, we're involved in conversation, having fun . . . and we've completely forgotten how bad we were feeling. We start by faking the emotion, and before long, the emotion becomes real.

"The secret of success is sincerity. Once you can
fake that, you've got it made."
— Jean Giraudoux

I can't tell you how many times before a performance I sit there and think, *Oh, God, not today!* Hey, I'm a human being—I don't always feel at my best, cheery and springy like Mary Poppins. Sometimes I'm just not in the mood to be funny, but since I'm paid to do so, and I wouldn't last too long in my career if I went onstage and started snapping at people like a crocodile, I fake it. I do whatever I need to do to psych myself up, and I force myself to get started. And unless I'm running a 103-degree fever, I'm having a good time and feeling like myself within minutes.

147

FAST TRACK TO FAKERY

When I'm in a lousy mood and feel like I just can't make myself get out there and do it, music gets me going. I put on my CD of Robert Palmer singing "Simply Irresistible"— and I picture the scene in the musical *Contact* where the song was used. It's an amazingly sexy and provocative number in which a beautiful young woman in a yellow dress dances with every guy in the place, and they all try to put on their best moves to impress her. The combination of the visualization and the music really makes me feel great—and helps get my

> blood moving and my brain snapping before a performance.
>
> What turns you on and gets you out of a bad mood? Music? Art? Poetry? Sex? Comedy? Sports? Pets? Kids? Think about it. . . .

Just Act As If

148

Whenever you start something new, you pretend you know what you're doing, right? But when the nurse puts your first baby into your arms at the hospital, do you suddenly become infused with all the knowledge of parenthood? Similarly, when you start a new job, do you immediately get promoted to supervisor? Of course not—for a long time, you simply act the part by pretending to know what you're doing. You do the best you can, and slowly you begin to feel comfortable with your new role in life. Going through the motions changes your psychology and helps you feel more and more comfortable. As I said, you fake it 'til you make it. You just show up, do your best, take responsibility, and the rest follows. . . .

The same techniques can be used to help you enhance your mood, bring more joy into your life, and help you wear your party pants every single day!

For example, if you're not feeling happy, fake it and see where that takes you. Paste a smile on your face, walk with your head held high, and force yourself to use body language that feigns enthusiasm and excitement. If you have to, skip, twirl, dance your way through the Gap . . . do anything you need to do to get your body out of a rut and into a place that feels like fun. You'll find that before long, you'll start to feel like you're having fun!

Suppose you're invited to a party and you're really feeling down. You want nothing more than to crawl back in bed and sit in front of the TV with a piece of pizza. The last thing in the world you want to do is be out there talking to people. Perhaps what you usually do is either not show up—or you do show up, but with an attitude that makes it clear you really wanted to stay home. You don't talk to anybody, sit down somewhere with a drink and stare out the window, or find some other way of staying unengaged.

But just this once, why not try forcing yourself to act as if you were one of those people who enjoy parties? Make believe it's a Broadway play, and you're the star: "Tonight! On this stage for the very first time, playing the role of someone who enjoys attending parties . . ."

What would someone who enjoys going to parties do? How would they stand? What would their body

149

language be like? What would they hold in their hands? What would their face look like—would they smile? Would they look into other people's eyes, or would they look away? Would they speak first? What would they say?

If you prepare for this night the way an actor prepares for a part, before long you'll start feeling much more comfortable in the role. For some people, it might happen immediately; for others, it might take many repeated tries. But playing the part over and over will make you feel much more comfortable, and it will help you convince yourself that you can play the part masterfully. You might even have some fun in the process!

150

LOOK INTO MY EYES . . .

Researchers have shown that when we gaze into someone else's eyes, we'll be inclined to like that person—*whether we have any other reason to or not.* So why aren't we gazing into everyone's eyes all the time?

You can use this technique to help you feel better in any aspect of your life. If you're timid, go into situations pretending to be bold. If you're bitter, go into situations pretending to be appreciative. If you're sad, pretend to be happy; if you're angry, pretend to be loving. It sounds simple—and in fact, it is! It's the simplest thing imaginable. Like everything else in life, it will take some time and effort to master. But the more you fake it, the more you'll create a pattern in your brain that tells you that whatever you're doing is achievable.

What's the Value?

When many of us don't show up, we're sending a signal that we need assistance; we're drowning and can't make human connections. It can be a call for help . . . but it's not an effective one, is it? By not showing up, we withdraw from the human community and make it nearly impossible for anyone to build a bridge. No one can help us if they don't know where we are. No matter what the excuse is for not showing up, the effect is that we're isolated, and other people feel slighted.

Just showing up—whether it means for others or for ourselves—means taking responsibility as a fellow inhabitant of this planet. It means being accountable for our actions and having the strength to allow other people to depend on us. It means being a little less narcissistic and a little more giving.

Living up to the values that we expect of ourselves—and that our friends and family members expect of us—lifts us to a higher level of existence. We never feel defensive, and we don't feel guilty for letting ourselves and other people down. Even if, going into a situation, we don't achieve everything we may have hoped for—knowing that we showed up and gave it a good try makes us feel good about ourselves. We feel that we can hold our head up high, and we deserve a place in the community around us.

152

It's a proven fact that people who attend support groups—everything from AA to Weight Watchers—have a much better chance of success if they attend meetings regularly, regardless of how vigilantly they follow the program rules. The simple act of showing up enhances any program's psychological power.

Are there issues or people in your life that you've been trying to avoid? Have you been ducking responsibility or accountability to someone or something? Don't set the bar too high: You don't need to mend broken relationships on the first try or finish a project you've been postponing for six months. Just show up. See what happens. Take responsibility—but not control. Things may very well start to sort themselves out on their own.

9

BUT WHAT DOES IT ALL MEAN?

"An amazing life requires meaning."

In the summer of 2001, I spent a week at the Chautauqua Institution near Buffalo, New York, and gave a talk for more than 6,000 people. I'd spoken there before, and had found myself quite enchanted with—and even inspired by—the concept of a place where attendees come together for a summer to learn, live in community, and find meaning in their lives. Getting to spend so much time with people who were on a quest for learning and purpose reminded me of just how important it is for each one of us to figure out what we're ultimately here to do. It ended up being one of the highlights of my career.

I was looking forward to my fall schedule, which was packed with wonderful engagements all over the country; however, during the week of September 11, I only had one. And so, on that fateful day, I was doing my usual busywork around the house when my husband called me to watch the horror that was occurring.

How quickly life changes. Lord knows how many of us found that our daily experiences immediately shifted from a sense of safety and security to one of dread and sadness. In a way, the tragedy happened to us all.

Similarly, I've met thousands of people who are going through chemotherapy; or who have lost children or significant others, homes, or financial security. They've shared their stories and their tears with me, always expressing their gratitude for my giving them an hour or two of laughter as a respite from their woes. And many of these individuals have shared how their work with me has helped them bring more meaning into their lives. When they thank me for what I've done for them, I say, "No, don't thank me. I want to thank *you* for showing me how you survive with strength, courage, and the ability to laugh in spite of tragedy."

What powerful examples they are for me! I try to think about them when I find myself "catastrophizing" about some minor irritation, such as a late airplane. These people have somehow learned how to reframe and reinterpret what's happened to them in order to

154

discover *more* of a reason to live, not less. Through sheer internal fortitude, they developed the strength to just keep looking for meaning, even when things seemed hopeless. Their ability to get to that point of revitalization and hope is something that should inspire each and every one of us. Ultimately, it's the only way to live our lives in a meaningful way.

Once again, I'd like to mention *Man's Search for Meaning*, for in it, Dr. Frankl asks us to answer this essential question: "Can we say yes to life in spite of everything?"

His query presupposes that life is meaningful under *any* conditions, even those that are the most miserable. And, in turn, it acknowledges the human capacity to creatively turn life's negative aspects into something positive or constructive. Frankl goes on to offer us his triad for tragic optimism:

1. Turning suffering into a human achievement and accomplishment.

2. Deriving from guilt the opportunity to change oneself for the better.

3. Deriving from life's transitory nature an incentive to take responsible action.

155

It's up to all of us to try to live our lives with more meaning, not only so that we can say yes to life, but so we may also say it to honor those who are no longer with us.

> *"This is the true joy in life, the being used for a purpose recognized by yourself as a mighty one; the being thoroughly worn out before you are thrown on the scrap heap; the being a force of Nature instead of a feverish, selfish little clod of ailments and grievances complaining that the world will not devote itself to making you happy."*
> — George Bernard Shaw

The Big Picture

I believe I knew my real purpose from the time I was a small child. I loved to make people laugh and feel good, and I loved doing things for those less fortunate than me. I'm sure that the latter comes from my Catholic school training with The Sisters of Perpetual Mood Disorders (no offense—really, I loved the nuns) where the study of altruism was always a part of the curriculum. The path toward sainthood was thought to be a noble pursuit, and many of my classmates and I romanticized it. (When you're young and innocent, you *do* get carried away. . . .) I've pared my desire to be canonized way down, but I was nevertheless left with a healthy sense of caring about others.

My childhood allowed me to be myself until my parents divorced when I was seven and my father became a nonparticipant in my life. After that, even when I did see him, he'd barely talk to me. I remember he never called me by name—he called me "girl," as in, "How old are you now, girl?"

For a few years after the divorce, my mother and I lived in Brooklyn with my grandparents—which was a delightful time for me. They were fun, they had neighbors in and out of their house all day long, they lived on a busy block where there were lots of kids, and my grandmother was a fabulous cook.

157

Then we moved to Long Island, and my life turned upside down. My mother remarried, and my stepfather was a very quiet individual . . . until something disturbed him, at which point he'd turn into a raving maniac. He also had long periods of unemployment that created anxiety for my mother. She took on the responsibility of keeping things going financially by, as she put it, "typing her brains out." Being her only child, I soon became her total focus. Her unhappiness over her second marriage drove her to want more and more for me and my future—and it turned her into an agent for the CIA. No matter what I did or who I was with, she investigated. She looked in my drawers, and read my letters *and* my journal (which was hidden under my mattress). Consequently, there were no boundaries in my life, no place for me to have a sense of self.

My mother was also highly critical, wanting me to be perfect in every way. I realize now that she was doing the best she could, but my young mind couldn't comprehend that—so I began to have panic attacks. I'd wake up in the middle of the night with heart palpitations, not knowing where I was. I only knew that I was scared out of my wits.

158

> *"There is no meaning to life except*
> *the meaning man gives to his life*
> *by the unfolding of his powers."*
> — Erich Fromm

The way I got through life was to use the gifts I was given: my humor, my zaniness, my sense of connecting to people, and my ability to see pain and suffering in others because I saw myself in them. Sometimes I'd sing a song, sometimes I'd tap dance—people would look at me and smile, and that made me feel good. I'd tell jokes, and others would laugh and want to be around me. That feeling of being engaged and appreciated saved my life. I loved to entertain!

I remember when I was only about six, I was taken to Radio City Music Hall, which, as you probably know, is an enormous show palace and movie theater in New York City. The movie playing that day was Disney's *Dumbo*. When the movie ended and all the kids started streaming out of the theater, I was miserable that this glorious experience had come to an end. So I ran to the front of the theater, in front of probably a couple of thousand people, and started yelling at the screen, "Dumbo, Dumbo, take me with you! Take me with you!" And all the people started to laugh, which is just what I wanted to happen.

I felt great.

When I look back on my life, it's clear that the moments that truly engaged me, that felt the most powerful and important, and that made me feel most connected with other people, had to do with performing, laughter, and lightheartedness. That's where the meaning in life lies for me. When a performance really "clicks"—when I'm lost in the energy of a show, the audience is responding, and I'm being creative—that's when I feel most alive. And when people say, "You helped to change my life," I'm in awe that I've been able to shift their perspectives.

159

But it wasn't always so apparent. For a long time, my ability to make people laugh and see absurdity in the mundane seemed like just another aspect of my personality. As I got older, it became clearer to me that this was where I found purpose, and it was the way for me to find meaning in my life and the world around me. I slowly began to make choices that honored that discovery, and soon I had a career *and* a life that were built around the things I found most meaningful—and the success that followed, both financially and spiritually, changed my life.

So where does meaning lie for *you?*

160

Map Out Your Life

Here's an exercise that I've seen my dear friend and colleague Dr. Ann Webster of the Mind/Body Medical Institute use to enormous success in her workshops.

Get yourself a huge sheet of paper—poster paper, if possible—and a box of markers or crayons. Starting at one end of the sheet, draw a road map of your life, with your birth as the starting point.

Draw it as if it were a highway. As you do, you'll probably find yourself only remembering major events. These can be landmarks, junctions, or detours. The landmarks may be easy to spot, or they may unfold as you re-create the journey. Make sure that you name the players in your life and how they helped or hindered you. Name the roads, towns, and so forth.

Now start to think deeper. Begin with your childhood—how did it feel? Who made a strong impression on you? Next, move on to your adolescence, school years, marriage, single parenthood (or just single status), illnesses, children, your choice of employment, tragedies, joys. . . . Can you find names for some of the roads on your particular map? Is there the Medical School onramp? The Twin Baby mountains? The Supercilious Supervisor detour?

Use different colors, stickers, glitter, or anything else that helps illustrate your defining moments. Hey, this is your life! So make it stand out and really show how you lived it.

When you've fitted your map with sufficient detail (and some people find that it's best to work on the map slowly, over the course of days or weeks, to really let the memories develop), it's time to look for the patterns that lead you to meaning. Do you find that certain behaviors, traits, talents, or passions recur at significant places on your map? If so, that's a signal that could lead toward your individual sense of meaning.

One woman I worked with found that her map was riddled with events having to do with music: a high school music teacher was a "traffic cop" who helped her find her way; a junction was the day she chose to attend business school instead of a performing arts school. Later in her life, a landmark was a classical music concert when Yo-Yo Ma performed in her town. She'd been so awed by the sound and beauty of the experience that she went out and bought dozens of albums.

I questioned her about the role of music in her life.

"I like music," she said, without enough energy to be really convincing.

"Like it?" I said.

"Well . . . I like it a lot. I often feel that when I listen to good music, problems wash away."

"So do you try to listen to music often?"

She shrugged. "When I can. There's not much time, with the kids and the housework and my job. I like long pieces—and I just can't take the time to listen to an hour-long symphony whenever I'd like."

I questioned the place on her map where she chose not to attend a performing arts school. It turned out that when she was young, she played the cello and was considered quite talented. But she didn't get much support from her family, who thought she needed to pursue a more traditional career.

"I really was pretty good," she said.

"Do you ever play now?"

"No—I don't even *own* a cello anymore. I haven't played for years. I don't think I could even remember the proper finger positions."

Sometimes she'd listen to music if her husband was working late and the kids were asleep. Her husband wasn't a big fan of classical music, and to get him to sit down with her and listen to a symphony was hardly worth the effort. He'd be bored by it, and she'd feel self-conscious and guilty . . . so she didn't even bother. Why is it that we often let our own passions go to appease others?

It became very clear to me, and soon to her, that the beauty and majesty of music was where she found meaning in life. Listening to fine classical music was when she felt most alive, energized, and emotional. She could often find herself in tears as she absorbed the beauty of a particularly intense moment of music.

"But what do I do with this now?" she asked. "I'm not about to leave my family and go to a conservatory somewhere!"

"Of course not," I said.

This woman was probably never going to play on the concert stage. She might, of course, if she opted to begin making choices that could lead her there—such as spending less time with her family and at work in order to study the cello. But it didn't sound to me as if that was what she wanted her life to be. She liked her

163

career, she loved her family, and she enjoyed things the way they were. She didn't want to change her entire life in order to pursue a career in music.

Many of us are stifled by the feeling that if we can't do something we love wholeheartedly and be the best in the world at it, then we shouldn't bother at all. We think that if we can't be Lance Armstrong, then we shouldn't be riding a bicycle. But God, how that cuts us out of so many of the wonders of life!

As for my friend the music enthusiast, there were so many ways for her to bring music into her life in a way that would enhance her sense of meaning. She and I discussed the possibility of her taking a course in music therapy or volunteering at a local hospital to organize a concert performance as a fund-raiser for cancer patients.

For this woman, there was something about music that she found transforming, peaceful, emotional, and powerful. Although she knew that it held meaning for her, she didn't realize that music truly was a *need* in her life—as important for her well-being as water and oxygen.

There are so many different places where human beings find meaning. For some, it's the appreciation of nature or of the arts—music, sculpture, theater; for others, it's an intellectual pursuit—mathematics, medicine, geology. Some people find it while engaging in sports or a creative act—painting, writing, composing music, photography; while many people find it in humanistic pursuits—parenting, friendship, helping the unfortunate. Oftentimes, the best of all worlds is when you can combine the humanistic with what brings you joy.

Map Out Your Future

Remember when I had you map out your past? Well, I'd like you to do it again—only this time, you'll be focusing on your future. Where do you want to go, and what do you want to do? Are there ways you can see yourself leaving a legacy that reflects your life's work? Are there dreams you've always wanted to realize?

165

I'm currently trying to create the last part of my journey. I want to help send my grandchildren to college. I also want to take singing lessons; travel to China; learn to speak Spanish; do some missionary work; and start an Institute of Health, Happiness, and Longevity.

I know from all that I've done with my life that "the thought does indeed manifest the deed." Therefore, not everything on your future map has to be of a lofty nature: If what you really want to do is take a trip to Las Vegas, write it down. But ultimately, it's those

things that speak to your higher self that will keep the
energy of life burning brightly within you.

Create a Library of Meaningful People and Share Them with Your Friends

Wouldn't it be wonderful to have a weekly salon,
like the kind that was prevalent during the Renaissance,
to talk about matters of interest? My favorite salon
(and probably the most famous) was the "Algonquin
Round Table." During the 1920s and '30s, Dorothy
Parker and a group of influential intellectuals gathered
weekly and discussed philosophy, psychology, the arts,
and whatever else turned them on.

Group discussion has a way of sharpening the
intellect, which is why I've always wondered why people spend so much time gabbing about negative and
unpleasant people and things. Wouldn't it be inspiring
to instead talk about individuals whose lives were filled
with meaning and who, indeed, brought more meaning to life for all of us? Some suggestions are: His
Holiness the Dalai Lama, Christopher Reeve, Martin
Luther King, Jr., Mother Teresa, Anne Frank, Eleanor
Roosevelt, Nelson Mandela, Maya Angelou, Winston
Churchill, and Rosa Parks.

166

Reflect and Review

In your search to find meaning, you may find that you know some pretty amazing people right in your own family who can help you. For example, I loved sitting down with my grandparents and asking about their lives, for to me, they were amazing people. My grandmother came to America at 21 years of age to reunite with my grandfather, who'd come ahead of her to make his fortune. This was in the days before the discovery of penicillin, and my grandfather had lost an arm as a result of an infection that now could be cured in a day. They were working-class people, and their lives were filled with struggle. Yet these were two of the most resilient people I've ever met; and their tenacity, strength, spirit, and humor taught me a lot about living a life with meaning.

Who can *you* learn from? How can their stories help you find your own path?

167

Making a Contribution

For most of us, the most powerful sense of meaning comes from doing something that makes us feel as if we're making a contribution to the world. Making a contribution connects us to our community, and society as a whole, in a way that makes us feel more fulfilled and essential. We feel better when we know that there's something we've done to help someone else, particularly when that person is in need. There's a reason that charity is an integral part of every world religion and most decent societies—helping other people is very clearly a vital component of life.

There are so many ways to make a difference. Many of us think that if we haven't singlehandedly developed a cure for cancer, then we haven't made a valuable contribution to the world. So, instead, we do nothing.

168

"When you have come to the edge of all the light
you know, and are about to step off into the
darkness of the unknown, faith is knowing one
of two things will happen: There will be
something solid to stand on,
or you will be taught to fly."
— Barbara J. Winter

You don't have to spend a year treating AIDS patients in Zimbabwe in order to make a valuable contribution to society. Spend an hour telling stories to a kindergarten classroom. Help clean up a city park. Serve on your PTA. Feed someone who can't hold a spoon. Visit a child in a hospital who has no one else to visit her. No matter what you do, connecting yourself to the community around you is a foolproof way to add meaning to your life.

For some people, meaning comes from a form of spiritual or religious belief. For them, feeling like part of a larger world that includes a divine presence—or a spiritual force—gives life true significance.

Spirituality is really all about meaning, isn't it? It's a way for us to understand our place in the world—indeed, our place in the *universe*. Religions help us see what's really important in life—there's not a lot of talk about cholesterol counts or SUVs in church.

So, look for the areas of your life that feel as if they're about more than just you and your daily existence. After all, life seems to be chock-full of detail and activity, and even things that make us feel good; but in the long run, it lacks meaning.

169

What are the things that make you feel connected to the universe, to being a human being? If looking at a building or a bridge makes you feel that kind of wonder, then perhaps you should be studying architecture—or at least reading about it now and then or going to exhibits at museums. If playing with a toddler makes you feel more connected to the universe, then you probably should be a teacher, or you should be spending some time volunteering at a day-care center or pediatric hospital.

Make choices that bring you closer to the things that hold meaning for you, and you'll find that your life is immeasurably happier and richer.

❈ ❈ ❈

10

JOIN THE PARTY!

"An amazing life requires connection."

Over the last several years, I've felt as if I've been going in two different directions. At work, I've lived in what seemed like a universal community. As I've mentioned, my nature is to be playful, and as such, I find it relatively easy to bond with just about anyone. I started to notice that when I was on the road, in touch with lots of people and exchanging stories, I started to look and feel years younger. The laughter, the intellectual stimulation, the awareness that there are many people leading lives that are far more difficult than mine—all of this has been a constant reminder that I'm blessed in many ways.

On the other hand, when I came home, I'd be exhausted and filled with a feeling of being dissociated from what I was saying and actually doing. I was, in essence, not living authentically. I'd be preaching about connection to the world—and I *would* connect with people for a short time when I was on the road—then I'd go home and hide so that I could be alone.

I realize now that part of this dichotomy resulted from the fact that I was so busy creating my career that I was totally exhausted, so I needed the quiet at home in order to regroup. Yet I was so sequestered at home that I rarely saw my family and friends. This may sound familiar to many of you, since it's become a common way of life in America.

Do we need time to be alone? Absolutely. But we can't live in such a divided way. My own attempts to try to solve this dilemma came unexpectedly—although that didn't surprise me, firm believer in synchronicity that I am.

As I mentioned previously, my mother recently moved in with me, and my entire life has turned upside down. She needs a lot of attention, so we hired Beatrice, a live-in care giver, to help her out. Beatrice is originally from Ghana, but she has now lived in this country for eight years.

And on top of all this, my husband retired.

All of a sudden, my once-quiet home has taken on the characteristics of a hotel lobby. There's always one TV blasting from my mother's room (she's hard of hearing) and another one (my husband's toy) blaring from the upstairs family room; people are constantly coming and going; and meal planning and scheduling doctors' appointments are now big parts of my daily experience.

Cooking meals and shopping for their ingredients are some of my mother's favorite activities. In fact, her first question when she wakes up is, "What's for dinner?" But before she arrived, my husband and I had fallen into a very laissez-faire way of dealing with meals. We often ate separately, whenever we felt like it. Let's just say that it wasn't something that took a lot of planning and preparation.

When my mother moved in, I felt as if aliens had invaded and were trying to suck the life out of me so that they could extend their own. However, as the days progressed, I found myself getting more and more accustomed to the intrusions. In fact, I started to really enjoy how much fun it was to talk to Beatrice at dinner, to ask questions about her country, her customs, and her life. Once I made peace with the fact that my mother's presence was going to be a permanent thing, I realized that this might be the way to heal the issues we had lingering from the past. And my husband's retirement has come in handy, too: When I'm on the road, he functions as the general manager of our "hotel."

In many ways, this situation has also provided me with what I felt was missing in my life. Prior to my mother's arrival, I'd been making a concerted effort to

173

spend more time connecting to my children and grand-children. I'm happy to say that has paid off. And so, with them coming and going—combined with the new commune that has become my home—it feels much more like the way I was brought up.

Believe me, we haven't turned into *Leave It to Beaver*. In fact, there are days when I feel more like Norman Bates from *Psycho*. But there's an energy now that was truly missing in my previous nice, orderly, peaceful existence. It's called *life*.

174

"Human connection is more than media and messages, information and persuasion; it also meets a deeper need and serves a higher purpose. Whether clear or garbled, tumultuous or silent, deliberate or fatally inadvertent, communication is the ground of meeting and the founda-tion of community. It is, in short, the essential human connection."

—*from The Human Connection* by Ashley Montagu

Most of us spend an enormous amount of time and energy keeping people at arm's length. I'll never understand this. Why don't we just say hello to our fellow travelers when we're on an elevator? They might not be receptive to the greeting, or they may look away or say something derisive—so what? Is it really worse than standing there in silence, pretending that we're alone? I can't think of much that feels lonelier than standing next to someone who isn't even acknowledging that I'm there.

But the most likely scenario is this one: They'll say something pleasant in return, you'll have a little smile and a friendly moment, and then you'll go on your way feeling just a little bit more connected to your fellow humans.

As I've said before, I talk to everybody. I always start chatting with the person sitting next to me on an airplane. And I know that the instant I open my mouth, they'll try to eye the stewardess to get their seat changed, even if I have no intention of gabbing all the way to Cleveland. I have a life, too, and I want to read, work, or take a nap on the plane, just like everybody else. But having a few moments of civil and entertaining conversation makes us both a little more human. I say something silly, and we'll have a little laugh. If the person happens to be a real dolt who won't engage with me, I'll just try harder. I find people who won't talk to me a challenge.

I never check out of the supermarket without saying something funny to the person working the register. I've had engaging and hilarious conversations with taxi drivers, hair stylists, bank tellers, and, you guessed it—people in elevators.

To me, not trying to connect is the opposite of engaging in life—it's isolating myself. If I don't talk to a taxi driver, then the only thing that defines our relationship is that fact that he's performing a service, driving me where I need to go—and we're both a little less human as a result of the encounter. Yet when we have a chat, it makes us both feel a little more connected and alive. And in the best of all worlds, I've learned something or had a little laugh.

176

HOWDY, NEIGHBOR!

It sounds simplistic, but a simple way to go back to a life of connection is to be more neighborly.

When's the last time you invited your neighbors over for a cup of coffee? That idea may even make you wince with discomfort—it's become almost corny to think of having pleasant interaction with the people next door. But in fact, this will make the area where you live more of a *community*—a place where people share interests and common courtesy, and give one another needed support and civility.

I know it might make you feel like Ozzie and Harriet, but if new neighbors move into the neighborhood, bring them a cake (make sure it's low-fat—you never know) or a handmade gift. Let them know that they're welcome by giving them your name and phone number, and offering to show them around town.

If one of your neighbors is ill, stop by and bring the family something to eat. These days, even those of us with good manners think that it's enough to send a card or some flowers. It isn't. Making a genuine effort coupled with some personal contact is what will really form a connection.

177

The Mentor Mentality

In my work, I've discovered that most people know at least one person who's had a profound effect on them, whether it be a teacher, family member, or colleague. For me, that person was my grandmother, Francesca.

My grandma wasn't a woman who would be particularly admired these days. It's unlikely that she'd be a guest on the *Today* show, or asked to pose for the cover of *Vanity Fair*. She was a proud, handsome woman of elegance and grace, who dressed with poise but not much flair.

However, she possessed a simple wisdom and an ability to see what a situation really called for, which was magnificent. It almost sounds silly now, but to my grandmother, a little red sauce could solve just about any problem that life had to offer. Somebody lost a job? "Ah, have some pasta. You'll feel better later." Heartbreak called for the big guns: a homemade zabaglione. And if one of us kids got hurt, first we'd get a kiss on the knee, then a little candy (the wrapper looking as if it had been through World War II) pulled from the bottom of her voluminous handbag.

These days we tend to think that Francesca's brand of homegrown remedies as simplistic and corny; but in fact, it's exactly her type of simplicity that today's world demands. How would you feel if, after a stressful day of work, commuting, children, phone calls, e-mail, and all the rest, you came home to Grandma? Instead of ordering Domino's, you'd sit down to a steaming hot plate of something delicious, as a loving voice said, "Here, I've made you a little something to eat." Sounds like heaven to me!

Is there somebody in your life who has had as profound an effect on you as Francesca had on me? If so, it's important to keep the energy of that relationship alive inside you in whatever ways you can. If that person is still alive, contact him or her. Even if it's someone you haven't seen in years, imagine how powerful it would be for an old teacher, employer, or friend to hear that you've been thinking of them for all these years. And maybe, just maybe, they'd still have wonderful, important, insightful things to add to your life. Perhaps they'll have the answers that will get you through.

If that person is no longer living, how can you keep their spirit alive? Maybe you could think of them when the going gets rough. Or put a photo of them on your desk or in your kids' bedroom. Is there a quote from them that's particularly poignant that you could print out and tape on your computer monitor or refrigerator?

179

HERE SHE COMES TO SAVE THE DAY!

A technique that I like to use with people when they're feeling isolated is "the Mighty Mouse technique." It's simple: When you're most in need of guidance, think of who has had the most profound effect on your life. Call them to come to your rescue—and, if you're feeling particularly whimsical, use the *Mighty Mouse* theme in your head: "Here I come to save the day."

What advice would that person give you? What would they do in the situation you're facing right now? Really get into it. Picture that person sitting next to you, advising you, and mentoring you. Envision them really standing beside you, telling you that you're doing the right thing and that they approve of the path you've chosen.

We really can't do it alone even though we wish we could. Life isn't meant to be lived in an isolated fashion. Human beings are bred to be together. For millions of years, we lived in tribes, and there was a good reason for that. Life is hard—we have to bring home food, create a household, raise the children, forge a community that protects itself, and on and on. And while our lives are now easier than they were for prehistoric people, it's still difficult for people and even families living in isolation. Our grandparents' generation knew that extended families should stay close by in order to help one another. People needed it.

There are many ways in which you can create that sense of community for yourself. Have you tried offering to bring your sibling's kids to school one or two days a week? And have you tried asking Mom if she'd like to watch your kids once a week? Can you offer to have dinner at your house for another family once a week, or once a month, and then you can go to their home a different day?

> *"Every thing that lives*
> *Lives not alone nor for itself."*
> — William Blake

181

SHARE GOOD NEWS

Researchers have discovered a fascinating phenomenon that highlights how important human connection is: If you perform an act of goodwill and altruism toward another person (such as assisting an elderly person across the street), it will give your immune system a boost. Even more interesting, though, is that someone simply *witnessing* the event will also get a boost.

That seems to indicate that even on the physical level, we're all influenced by each other's dialogues and actions—that by simply being part of someone else's good mood and deeds, our own mood and spirit will be elevated.

A way to make this work for you is to use the technique of sharing good news. Now, most of us find it enormously uncomfortable to tell others about something positive we've done, or something we're happy about or proud of. We tend to undermine the good and highlight the negative, don't we? We say, "Yes, I've won the Pulitzer Prize, but God, I've got the thighs of a heifer!" or "Thanks so much for the compliment, but you're looking at the zit on the tip of my nose right now, aren't you?" We're so uncomfortable saying good things that we have to temper them with negativity.

182

What you do in this exercise is this: Grab another person, and take turns telling one another things that make you feel good about yourself. Simply force yourself to tell good news, *without tempering it with negative words*. One person talks while the other listens. The listener must, even if they don't feel it, show interest and excitement. Then switch places.

If two people do this for any extended period of time, they'll create a little bubble of good spirit around themselves that, even if it feels completely unnatural in the beginning,

> will grow into genuine goodwill and emotional bonding. We make one another feel good when *we* feel good; our moods are contagious, uplifting, and enlightening. And sharing our good moods creates bonds between people that are a constant resource for more good moods.

In the days following September 11, 2001, all over the country and especially in New York City (for obvious reasons), there was an amazing outpouring of kindness. I heard from my friends in the city that for several weeks there was incredible cooperation and decency among people in the street, in the elevators, and even on the subways. People were looking one another in the eye and making small talk. Everyone talked about where they were that morning, what they saw, and whom they knew among the missing. We were bound by the experience, and in a strange and sad way, it made the world a nicer place for a few weeks.

Why does it take a tragedy for people to be kind to one another? Why should it take death and destruction for people to feel comfortable talking to one another in public places? We're all in this journey together; on the good days and on the tragic ones, too. How much nicer a world this would be if we could all remember that.

*"Let us make one point, that we meet each other
with a smile, when it is difficult to smile.
Smile at each other, make time for
each other in your family."*
— Mother Teresa

Think of all the little ways in which you truly honor the people who are in your life now—ways in which you can demonstrate that the relationship is important to you and that you'd like to deepen the connection.

184

I hate the phrase *quality time* because it's a contemporary cliché, and also because I think it undermines the reality of relationships. Shouldn't *all* time together be quality time—and if it isn't, then what the hell is non-quality time? Do I really need to schedule special time with my kids in order to respect our relationship?

It seems to me that what really makes time "quality" or not has nothing to do with where you go or what you do. Quality time doesn't have to be at an expensive amusement park with your kids or at a four-star restaurant with your girlfriends. The thing that makes time with others special is *focus* and *attention*.

These days, even when we're spending time with people, we're multitasking and doing three other things at once. We're on our way to or from another errand;

we're expecting a call; we're preparing a meal for someone else; we're typing on our computer while we're
talking to a friend on the phone.

Nurturing a relationship takes focus and attention, the hallmarks of respect. How can someone feel
that we respect them if we're doing something else at
the same time, constantly looking at our watch because
we need to get somewhere?

Show the people in your life that you respect them
and honor their love and affection by giving them your
full attention, even if it's only for a small fraction of the
day. If you're playing a game with your kids in the
evening, turn off the phone for a while, or let it ring.
Let your kids feel that this is *their* time, that they're the
most important thing in the world to you in that
moment and that everything else can wait.

When you're having lunch with a friend, turn off
your cell phone. Don't talk about other demands or
where you have to be in 15 minutes. Don't let outside
pressures intrude on your time together. I find these
days that the first 15 minutes of every conversation I
have with someone seems to be taken up with chatter
about how busy we all are. For me, that kind of talk
takes all the energy out of the moment. It makes me
feel as if I'm intruding on that person's day—that I'm
either getting in the way of their doing some work or

185

getting some rest. I don't want to be an intruder; I want to be a fellow celebrant!

TEN SIMPLE WAYS
TO CONNECT TODAY

1. Smile at someone in the elevator.

2. Invite a co-worker to lunch.

3. Call your mother, or someone in your life who nurtures you.

186

4. Give someone a compliment— and mean it.

5. Make small talk with the person who sells you your morning coffee.

6. Make a funny face in an unexpected place (like in line at the supermarket) until someone laughs.

7. *Talk* to your family during dinner, without any outside distractions.

8. Call someone you haven't spoken to in a year.

9. Give someone in your life a gift, for no special reason other than that you think they might like it.

10. Tell people that you appreciate what they do for you—perhaps your local firefighters or police officers. Wouldn't they be shocked to have people drop by to say, "Thank you for being there in case we need you"?

Human beings are our companions and our community. Life is only the big party it was meant to be if there are other people there, dancing, singing, chatting, and making waves right there alongside of you. Draw more people into your life, and the party will just get better . . . and more interesting, varied, lively, and fun.

187

Allow yourself to connect with kindness, compassion, empathy, and good humor—let your hair down, put on your party pants, and celebrate your life!

I'll have a noisemaker waiting for you.

❋ ❋ ❋

ABOUT THE AUTHOR

Loretta LaRoche is an internationally known stress-management consultant who advocates humor as a coping mechanism. She uses her wit and wisdom to help people learn how to take stress and turn it into strength, and how to see themselves as the survivors of their own lives—that is, to find the "bless in the mess."

Loretta is a favorite with viewers of her five PBS specials; as well as on the lecture circuit, where she presents an average of 100 talks per year. She's the author of *Relax, You May Only Have a Few Minutes Left* and *Life Is Not a Stress Rehearsal,* among other works. She lives in Plymouth, Massachusetts. Website: **LorettaLaroche.com**

Hay House Titles
of Related Interest

Books

Getting Unstuck, by Dr. Joy Browne

Gratitude, by Louise L. Hay and Friends

How to Ruin Your Life, by Ben Stein

Inner Peace for Busy People, by Joan Z. Borysenko, Ph.D.

Little Things Make a Big Difference, by Laurin Sydney

Meditation, by Brian L. Weiss, M.D. (book-with-CD)

10 Secrets for Success and Inner Peace,
by Dr. Wayne W. Dyer

Turning Inward: A Private Journal for Self-Reflection,
by Cheryl Richardson

Wisdom of the Heart, by Alan Cohen

Card Decks

I Can Do It® Cards, by Louise L. Hay

If Life Is a Game, These Are the Rules, by
Chérie Carter-Scott, Ph.D.

Until Today, by Iyanla Vanzant

Women's Bodies, Women's Wisdom Healing Cards,
by Christiane Northrup, M.D.

Words of Wisdom for Women Who Do Too Much,
by Anne Wilson-Schaef

All of the above are available at your local bookstore,
or may be ordered through Hay House, Inc.,
at the numbers on the last page.

NOTES

NOTES

NOTES

NOTES

NOTES

NOTES

NOTES

NOTES

We hope you enjoyed this Hay House book.
If you would like to receive a free catalog featuring additional
Hay House books and products, or if you would like
information about the Hay Foundation, please contact:

Hay House, Inc.
P.O. Box 5100
Carlsbad, CA 92018-5100

(760) 431-7695 or (800) 654-5126
(760) 431-6948 (fax) or (800) 650-5115 (fax)
www.hayhouse.com

Published and distributed in Australia by:
Hay House Australia, Pty. Ltd. • 18/36 Ralph St. • Alexandria NSW
2015 • *Phone:* 612-9669-4299 • *Fax:* 612-9669-4144
• www.hayhouse.com.au

Published and distributed in the United Kingdom by:
Hay House UK, Ltd. • Unit 62, Canalot Studios •
222 Kensal Rd., London W10 5BN • *Phone:* 44-20-8962-1230 •
Fax: 44-20-8962-1239 • www.hayhouse.co.uk

Published and distributed in the Republic of South Africa by:
Hay House SA (Pty), Ltd., P.O. Box 990, Witkoppen 2068 •
Phone/Fax: 2711-7012233 • orders@psdprom.co.za

Distributed in Canada by:
Raincoast • 9050 Shaughnessy St., Vancouver, B.C. V6P 6E5 •
Phone: (604) 323-7100 • *Fax:* (604) 323-2600

Sign up via the Hay House USA Website to receive the
Hay House online newsletter and stay informed about what's
going on with your favorite authors. You'll receive bimonthly
announcements about: Discounts and Offers, Special Events,
Product Highlights, Free Excerpts, Giveaways, and more!
www.hayhouse.com